HORIZON

JANUARY, 1977 · VOLUME XIX, NUMBER 1

CONTENTS

PERSPECTIVES

COURTESY AUDREY TOPPING

COVER: After more than two thousand years underground, this armored Chinese warrior is uncovered and measured in a rock vault near the tomb of China's first emperor. Almost six feet tall and wearing a cap that may denote high rank, the soldier is part of a major new discovery. (See article overleaf.)

EDITORIAL

In Our Own Image

Chairman Mao   Ch'in Shih Huang

Not long ago, near the ancient Chinese city of Sian in Shensi province, some farmers drilling for water came upon what has proved to be one of the most amazing treasures ever unearthed: a veritable army of life-sized pottery statues and other objects, buried some 2,200 years ago by order of the first emperor of China, Ch'in Shih Huang. So far as we know, the only Western journalist who has visited the excavation site is Audrey Topping. Her account of what she saw there will be found overleaf, together with a selection of photographs provided by the Chinese government—the first full-scale report and the first photographic coverage to appear in the American press.

The pottery army is near the emperor Ch'in's tomb (yet to be investigated), and Mrs. Topping compares the discovery to that of Tutankhamen's tomb in 1922. In some respects it is even more important, for the young Pharaoh—however magnificent his grave goods—was not a figure of great significance, whereas Ch'in Shih Huang changed the course of Chinese history, like his latter-day successor Mao Tsetung, who often compared himself with Emperor Ch'in.

What the Chinese archaeologists have found is startlingly rich in quality and quantity, but that is not all there is to say of it. The emperor Ch'in lived in a remote and conflict-filled epoch in a land that to most Americans is still terra incognita. Yet to look at these ancient objects resurrected from the earth is to be struck with their familiarity, their humanity. Here are hundreds of statues, each one a faithful portrait of a man. The written record (and a highly unreliable one it is) says that

Ch'in Shih Huang was a merciless tyrant who sacrificed untold numbers of laborers on such megalomaniacal projects as the Great Wall. Yet, in a time when no one would have thought it very odd if the emperor had merely buried the guardsmen themselves alive to have a showy funeral, why did he bother to immortalize the members of his imperial guard? What other potentate has endowed posterity with so many faces from the past?

Elsewhere in this issue is an article on another kind of exploration — the adventure into space. The possibility that civilized life exists outside our solar system has tantalized astronomers for years, and there is, in fact, a plan afoot at this moment to build a gigantic radio transmitter called Cyclops to detect and send interstellar messages. But in "Conversations among the Galaxies" (page 48), Ronald Bracewell of Stanford University has come up with a more practical suggestion. Reasoning that whoever is Out There is likely to be more technologically advanced than we, he predicts that *they* may discover *us*. While waiting for their space probe to arrive (it will have no passengers), we should try to figure out how to get the conversation going and decide what questions we want to ask.

Professor Bracewell, like most astronomers and exobiologists, chooses to believe that our extragalactic companions will turn out to be more or less like us. The designers of the recent Mars probe were not looking for bizarre new chemicals but the basic elements of life on Earth—hydrogen, oxygen, nitrogen, carbon. So strong is this belief that exobiologists Carl Sagan and Frank Drake of Cornell (who advocate that *we* should be trying to discover *them*) propose that we broadcast, as part of the opening gambit from Cyclops, a model of the double helix and the chemical composition of DNA. Some creature built of triangular silicone cells may decode the message and laugh, but until we encounter such monstrosities, what else indeed can we expect to find, either at the bottom of an excavation pit in China, or in another solar system, except something made in our own image?

Carl Sagan has recently written that the success of the human species is due in large part to our passion for exploration. Whether the voyage goes into an ancient tumulus or beyond the galaxy, or inside a work of art and the mind of its creator, the voyagers are certain to be looking for news about human life and human nature—news, that is, about ourselves. Wherever these explorations get under way, HORIZON will be aboard, keeping the logbook. —S.T.

AMERICAN HERITAGE PUBLISHING COMPANY

CHAIRMAN OF THE BOARD
Samuel P. Reed

PRESIDENT AND PUBLISHER
Rhett Austell

EDITOR IN CHIEF, MAGAZINES: Alvin M. Josephy, Jr.
SENIOR EDITORS: Joseph J. Thorndike, Oliver Jensen
CONSULTING EDITOR: J. H. Plumb
EDITORIAL ART DIRECTOR: Murray Belsky

TREASURER: Anthony J. Sansiveri
PROMOTION DIRECTOR: Ernest Quick
PROMOTION ART DIRECTOR: David Van Inwegen
CIRCULATION AND SALES DIRECTOR: Donald B. Barrows, Jr.
PRODUCTION DIRECTOR: Elbert Burr

EDITOR: Shirley Tomkievicz
MANAGING EDITOR: Priscilla Flood   ART DIRECTOR: Kenneth Munowitz
ARTICLES EDITOR: Charles E. McLaughlin
SENIOR ASSOCIATE EDITOR: Mary Sherman Parsons   FEATURES EDITOR: Susan Ferris
ASSOCIATE EDITOR: Mary Z. Jenkins   ASSISTANT EDITOR: Marya Dalrymple
EDITORIAL ASSISTANTS: Arthur S. Hayes, Allan Ripp
CONTRIBUTING EDITORS: Walter Karp, Barbara Klaw   COPY EDITOR: Kendra K. Ho
ASSISTANT TO THE EDITOR: J. Muriel Vrotsos   ROVING EDITOR: Frederic V. Grunfeld
CHIEF, EUROPEAN BUREAU: Gertrudis Feliu, *11 rue du Bouloi, 75001 Paris*
LONDON EDITOR: Christine Sutherland, *51 Victoria Road, London W8*

ADVISORY BOARD: Gilbert Highet, *Chairman*, Frederick Burkhardt,
Charles L. Mee, Jr., John Pfeiffer, John Walker

HORIZON is published six times a year by American Heritage Publishing Co., Inc. Editorial and executive offices: 10 Rockefeller Plaza, New York, N.Y. 10022. Treasurer and Secretary: Anthony J. Sansiveri. All correspondence about subscriptions should be addressed to: HORIZON Subscription Office, 381 West Center St., Marion, Ohio 43302.

Single copies: $5.00. Subscriptions: $26.00 per year in the U.S.; Canada and elsewhere: $28.00.
Hard-cover edition: Single copies: $7.50. Subscriptions: $32.00 per year in the U.S.; Canada and elsewhere: $34.00.

Cumulative indexes for Volumes I–V, VI–X, and XI–XV are available at $7.50. HORIZON is also indexed in the *Readers' Guide to Periodical Literature*. The editors welcome contributions but can assume no responsibility for unsolicited material. Title registered U.S. Patent Office. Second-class postage paid at New York, N.Y., and at additional mailing offices.

LETTERS

Budapest, 1956

Stephen Vizinczey ["Memoirs of a Freedom Fighter," Autumn, 1976] was a student when he fought the Russian tanks in the streets of Budapest. Twenty years after the Hungarian revolt, he is still young at heart: firm in his youthful belief that great wrongs can, must, and, eventually, will be righted; that people will not allow foreigners to run their lives forever; that the Hungarians will again rebel against their oppressor. He justifies his optimism historically. For him, the 1956 revolt against the mighty Soviet Union, although a folly, was no temporary aberration: "it is a national trait."

Uncompromising patriotism is an important historical myth, one that helps nations to stay alive in adversity, but a myth that has rarely been translated into reality. . . . The Hungarian nation revolted in 1956 because the Soviet occupation had been more evil and stupid than any previous occupation; it was worse even than the Soviet occupation in other East European countries. But, after 1956 the Soviets learned their lesson, and so did the Kremlin's Hungarian emissaries. As a result, the Hungarian nation is no longer in revolt; instead, it goes about its business with astonishing ease. . . .

Their willingness to submit to the strong no more sets the Hungarians apart than their occasional outburst of patriotic heroism and suicidal self-sacrifice. Certainly some Hungarians still look back to Hunyadi or to Zrinyi, but many more Hungarians no longer bother to look back to anything. They prefer to look ahead, and what they see is not a brave cavalry charge, but an automobile, a summer house, and a vacation. Today when Secretary Kissinger wishes that the Soviet Union be allowed to "digest" her East European conquest undisturbed, such an outlook doubtless has its merit.

Istvan Deak
Columbia University
New York, New York

．　．　．

What Stephen Vizinczey fails to mention is that all Hungarian revolutions started with an outburst of emotions rather than with battle plans. All were based on, and doomed by, appalling misconceptions and vain hopes for foreign help. The pathos of "Budapest, 1956" was that the revolutionaries assumed that the Russians would go home.

Moreover, two totally opposed, inimical groups of Hungarians prepared for the revolt. College students and young intellectuals, many of them sincere, idealistic socialists, started wildly demonstrating for reforms, and suddenly all of yesteryear's fascists, Nazis, or simply hangers-on from the dissolved Horthy regime saw their chance of riding piggyback on this outbreak. Rumors circulated that U.S. Army divisions in Bavaria were preparing to intervene. But the Yanks were *not* coming. And although the hero of the moment, Imre Nagy, was full of good intentions, he was short on leadership. So the fate of the revolt was sealed.

While Mr. Vizinczey's poetic prose is moving, it has little to do with the facts of Hungarian life. Disappointing fact will not, of course, tarnish personal heroism nor the tragedy, only somewhat dim the halo of martyrdom wrought by miscalculation and inexperienced leadership.　Gabriel D. Hackett
New York, New York

The Conquest of Siberia

Timothy Severin ["How Siberia Was Won," Autumn, 1976] is far more cautious than most people in judging the value of Siberia as a conquest; he emphasizes its immense size, one-tenth of the world's land surface. Many Russians and even more foreigners insist on Siberia's supposedly infinite riches, and speculate wildly about its future as the center of Russia's population, industry, and power. Yet, compared to the hopes Russian governments have had of it, Siberia is the world's most colossal flop.

One problem is getting there and back. Siberia's famous river system was backbreaking enough if you were a Cossack in a riverboat. It was more brutal and more frustrating if you were Sergei Witte or Joseph Stalin faced with the tasks of laying out dozens of discontinuous summer-only steamboat routes, and of replacing them with tens of thousands of miles of wilderness railroads and dirt truck roads. Siberia has

HORIZON welcomes comments and questions from readers. Letters should be addressed to The Editor, HORIZON, 10 Rockefeller Plaza, New York, New York 10020.

famous supplies of coal and iron—fifteen hundred miles apart—so Siberia has, famously, the highest materials-cost steel industry in the world.

Moscow has found Siberia annoying from the start. When Siberia meant a wealth of furs, the czars were chagrined to find that the Dutch merchants who picked up the furs at Russian ports made three times as much money out of them as all the Russian trappers, merchants, and tax collectors combined. When the empress Elizabeth, the Holy Whore, instituted the Siberian exile system as a "humane" substitute for executing criminals, something went wrong with the image of humaneness.

Wise Russians illustrate the promise and disappointment of Siberia with the traditional tale of the peasant from Barnaul who traveled to the court of the mad czar Paul, in 1796, in order to display his invention, a strange contraption of wheels and cylinders that sputtered and popped, a kind of cart that drove the peasant round the ballroom floor without a horse, powered, the peasant claimed, only by some stuff he had distilled from a nearby oil spring. The czar was impressed and gave the peasant a small bag of gold, and sent him and his automobile back to Siberia, where they were never heard of again.　Francis Randall
Sarah Lawrence College
Bronxville, New York

Dracula: The Balkan Fu Manchu

I wish to congratulate Walter Karp for his analysis of the resurrection of the vampire in this century ["Dracula Returns," Autumn, 1976], especially in the cinema. But I do think that Karp somewhat neglects the charismatic persona of Lugosi himself in explaining Dracula's popularity. At the height of his career, Lugosi was accorded superstar status; he received multiple marriage proposals from the female fans who had fallen under his cinematic sway. And while Karp cogently outlines the sociohistorical origins for the vampire's rise in the West, I would add that Bram Stoker was very much the child of his colonializing, intensely xenophobic Victorian culture. Stoker perceived Dracula as a kind of Balkan Fu Manchu, threatening the order of the English "civilized" world with a vampire horde concealed in fifty coffins.

Harvey R. Greenberg, M.D.
New York, New York

One of the most spectacular archaeological finds since the discovery in 1922 of King Tutankhamen's tomb near Luxor was made three years ago when Chinese peasants drilling a well in the Yellow River valley found a tunnel strewn with pottery figures of soldiers and horses. Excavations soon revealed the existence of a buried army consisting of more than six thousand terra-cotta figures of armed soldiers, servants, and horses drawing war chariots arrayed in battle formation. All are approximately life-size, all have different facial characteristics, and all were created more than two thousand years ago to guard the tomb of China's great unifier and first emperor, Ch'in Shih Huang Ti, who reigned from 221 to 210 B.C.

The first discoveries were made in the spring of 1974, and excavations began in 1975. The site, near the ancient capital city of Sian in Shensi province, lies about four thousand feet east of the actual tomb mound of Emperor Ch'in, which, according to ancient writings, is guarded against intruders by traps and automatically triggered weapons.

In contrast to the publicity that accompanied the findings of Tutankhamen's tomb, Sian officials, with standard Chinese understatement, modestly announced their discovery abroad in the *Peking Review*, a government periodical, and transmitted a few black-and-white photos to foreign news agencies.

When excavation of the Egyptian Pharaoh's tomb began, royalty, foreign dignitaries, and eager reporters from all over the world arrived in Luxor to follow the archaeological proceedings. In China, at least initially, no foreigners were allowed to visit the area and few details of the find were released. I was the first Western journalist to see the excavation site near Sian and to talk to archaeologists involved in the project.

This area of Shensi province in the Yellow River valley is where China's civilization began thousands of years ago and where the earliest emperors lived and died. From the time Ch'in Shih Huang Ti established the Mandate of Heaven in 221 B.C., until the fall of imperial rule in 1911, the emperors of China believed they reigned by divine right over the "center of the universe." Now the area around Sian is an archaeologist's paradise with hundreds of imperial tombs filled with royal riches and art treasures waiting to be excavated. The most wondrous of these tombs will undoubtedly prove to be that of Ch'in Shih Huang Ti, who used hundreds of thousands of forced laborers and spent thirty-eight years constructing a subterranean palace in which to spend eternity.

It had been raining heavily for weeks when we arrived in Sian in October, 1975, and museum officials were reluctant to take us to the site because work had been suspended and they were afraid we would get too wet. We pleaded with them to take us in spite of the rain. After hours of indecision, during which we consumed a nine-course lunch, the convoy of cars that had met us at the airport appeared and we were off.

About twenty miles out of Sian we turned off the paved road and followed a dirt cart path through a millet field edged with persimmon trees. In the middle of the field the earth had been opened to reveal China's past in a dramatic tableau. Looking

By AUDREY TOPPING

Clay Soldiers:

The Army of Emperor Ch'in

He was the ruler who built the Great Wall
and unified China—the
emperor Chairman Mao most admired.
Now the greatest of his works
is emerging from the past in an extraordinary
archaeological discovery

On a recent trip to China, Audrey Topping, above right, poses with her father, Chester Ronning (former Canadian envoy to Nanking), and a Chinese friend. Mrs. Topping, who has visited China six times, was the first Western journalist to visit the site near Sian (on the map below), where the magnificent warriors that guard Emperor Ch'in's tomb are being excavated. One of them, opposite, has just been unearthed.

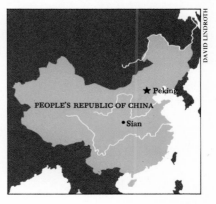

Several hundred soldiers—a phalanx of men armed with swords, crossbows, and spears—have been discovered so far. Some 2,200 years old, each figure is a unique portrait of one of the emperor's hand-picked honor guard. Impassive, fierce, or half-smiling, the warrior's faces, above, reveal a remarkable variety, as do the mustaches, beards, and elaborate coiffures in the drawings below of excavated heads.

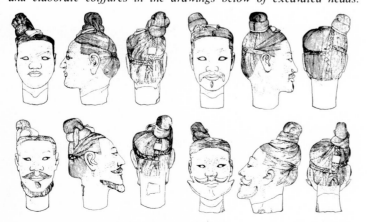

into the pit at the recently unearthed terra-cotta figures was like looking back more than two thousand years at an ancient battlefield. There, half buried in the reddish earth, were the hundreds of battered, beautiful sculptured figures, all astonishingly realistic. That day they appeared very lifelike because the flesh-and-gray-toned fired clay glistened from the pouring rain.

We stood in stunned silence, overwhelmed by the beauty and dignity of the figures emerging from the rough, wet earth after 2,200 years of burial. Some figures were almost completely unearthed and stood as if poised to attack; others were half buried, or smashed and scattered. Here and there a hand stretched eagerly out of the earth. Proud heads, fallen from broken bodies, looked up from their centuries-old grave, their fierce eyes fixed on us.

No two figures look alike because each is a portrait of a real person. They were modeled after the emperor's own warriors, servants, and footmen. The soldiers are distinguished by hip-length vests fashioned out of clay to look like armor, which are worn over high-necked, knee-length tunics and trousers or leggings. Most of them sport jaunty mustaches or Fu Manchu beards. Their sculpted hair is parted in the middle and pulled back in different types of knots.

The legion is arrayed in battle formation, just as the emperor's live honor guard was actually aligned before it set off on a military campaign. All of them once carried real swords, spears, and crossbows. All were buried in a standing position. The servants and footmen have no armor, but wear high-necked garments that fasten across the chest and reach the knees over baggy knickers. Only a hint of the original color painted on the pottery clothing remains. Their ankle boots are also laced and tied in bows. Like the soldiers, their hair is parted in the middle; some are bareheaded, while others wear various types of headdress. All stand about six feet tall. They look as alive today as they did when they were first created: some fierce, others proud and confident. A few seem on the verge of smiling.

The horses stand four abreast before their royal war chariots. Some are incredibly whole, others have broken backs and necks, but all are magnificent. The horses' elaborate leather harnesses have almost disappeared. Only a few brass links and chariot fixtures remain, and the imperial funerary chariots, which were made of wood, are now mostly charred imprints in the earth. Wood and leather could not survive the fire set by hostile invaders three years after the death of the emperor.

At the time I visited the site, 591 warriors, 24 horses, and 4 chariots had been excavated. This is just a beginning. The archaeologists at the dig think the whole army consists of a phalanx of some six thousand figures, buried in a vault fifteen to twenty feet deep and occupying some seven hundred feet by two hundred feet. The immense chamber used to be lined with bricks, and the ceiling was once supported by giant wooden columns. An elaborate hall had been erected over the vault to hide its existence.

Now, five sloping passageways lead to the pit where workers

COURTESY LUCY LIM; LEFT: COURTESY AUDREY TOPPING; CENTER, TOP AND BOTTOM: *Wen Wu*, NOVEMBER, 1975

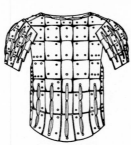

Ch'in dynasty armor was made of metal plates overlapped, above and left, or stitched to a tunic, below. The unarmored life-size foot soldier, right, wears a kimonolike robe.

have also unearthed more than a thousand relics, including swords, arrowheads, and iron farm tools, treated before burial with a chemical preservative that enabled them to remain uncorroded for more than twenty centuries. Gold, jade, bamboo, and bone artifacts, linen, silks, bronze and pottery utensils, and bronze wires in different sizes have also been found.

Prior to the discovery of this huge cache of Ch'in sculptures and artifacts, our knowledge of the art of this period was practically nonexistent. Now we have substantial proof that, in both form and subject, the Ch'in sculptures mark a significant and dramatic departure from earlier Chinese art. Bronze vessels from the Shang and Chou dynasties, which spanned the eighteenth to the third centuries B.C., were often embossed with forms of mythical beasts, semiabstract monster masks, and animal motifs. The decorations on these ritual containers indicate an obsession with symbolism and the supernatural. In contrast, the human and equestrian Ch'in figures reveal a strong concern for realistic detail and for the real world.

Credit for this dramatic breakthrough from the abstract to the real in Chinese art was previously given to artists of the Han dynasty (202 B.C.–A.D. 220), which followed the Ch'in. (Han realism was vividly demonstrated by a series of bronze horses in the exhibition of relics from the People's Republic of China that toured the United States in 1975.) But the extraordinarily realistic figurines of the Han are now rivaled, both in size and artistic value, by the earlier and more original Ch'in figures from the emperor's tomb.

•   •   •

From 481 to 221 B.C. China was split into warring feudal states. In 259 B.C. Cheng Wang was born prince of the state of Ch'in. After his father died in 246 B.C., he ascended the throne at the age of thirteen and spent his next twenty-five years in battle. According to Ssŭ-ma Ch'ien, the "Herodotus of China," who lived from 145 to 86 B.C., he conquered all of China "like a silkworm devouring a mulberry leaf." In 221 B.C. he unified the states under a central government and declared

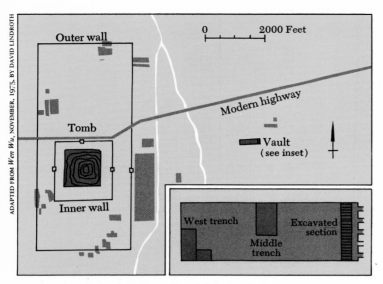

ADAPTED FROM *Wen Wu*, NOVEMBER, 1975, BY DAVID LINDROTH

The emperor's tomb and the vault for his army

Ch'in Shih Huang's tomb, which lies beneath the mound opposite, was built within two vast enclosures (see plan above). About four thousand feet to the west of the tomb lies the underground vault for the imperial guard. The section already excavated and the exploratory trenches are indicated in the inset map above. Below, in the detailed diagram of the excavated area, are the eleven corridors that have been uncovered. In all of them, life-size figures (now tumbled and disarrayed) were interred in battle formation. Corridors 2, 3, 5, 7, 9, and 10 contain horses and chariots, each carrying two passengers and accompanied by foot soldiers. In corridors 4, 6, and 8 were found ranks of warriors that once stood eight abreast. At the top of the diagram are three rows of warriors, seventy-two to a row. In corridors 1 and 11, along the north and south sides of the vault, are double rows of soldiers facing outward. According to ancient chronicles, soothsayers guided Ch'in Shih Huang's generals in the planning of what was intended to be a propitious battle formation.

himself Ch'in Shih Huang Ti (*Shih* meaning "the first," *Huang Ti*, "sovereign emperor"). Huang Ti remained the title of all imperial rulers in China until the downfall of the Manchu dynasty in 1911. (Today the Chinese have dropped the Ti and call him Ch'in Shih Huang.)

Ch'in Shih Huang is best remembered for his construction of the Great Wall, built to protect the newly formed empire from nomadic barbarians living north on the Mongolian steppes. (The ancient proverb "Have no fear of tigers from the south, but beware even a rooster from the north" later proved well founded.) The emperor used a forced labor crew—prisoners of war and criminals. They joined existing walls and ramparts, built earlier by feudal states for protection from one another's armies, and extended them about fifteen hundred miles over precipitous mountaintops, valleys, and plains. Thousands of these unfortunate men perished, their bones crushed and buried beneath the massive gray rocks—giving the wall the grim epithet "the longest cemetery in the world." But this, the world's longest fortification, has survived the centuries and was the only mark made by man on earth that the astronauts could see from space.

Ch'in Shih Huang's reign over unified China, which is known today as the Ch'in dynasty, lasted only eleven years, but in that time he made the sweeping changes that make his dynasty a turning point in the history of China. By destroying the ancient feudal system and establishing a centralized monarchy, he radically altered the political and social structure of the state. He standardized weights and measures as well as the system of writing, so that the Chinese language could be read and understood in all parts of the empire. He built a vast

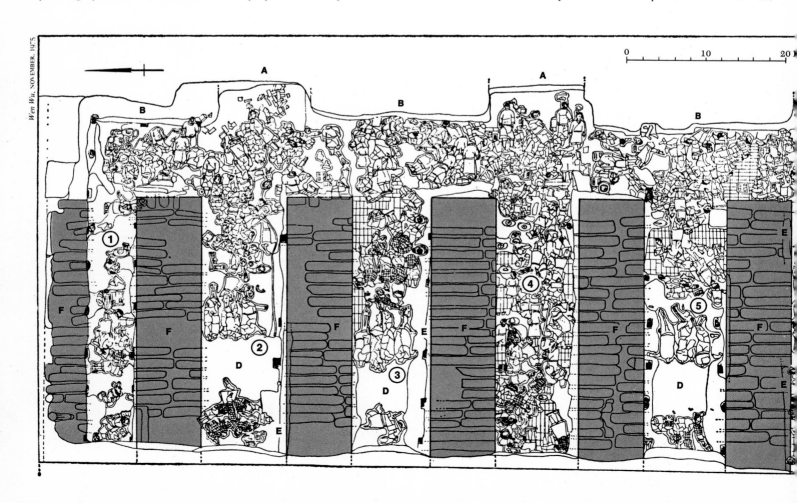

Wen Wu, NOVEMBER, 1975

Mount Li, the emperor Ch'in's tomb mound, has yet to be explored.

network of roads and joined the rivers by a series of canals, some still in use today. This vast inland communications system made possible the transport of food and other essential goods to and from all parts of the empire. And a new method of irrigation introduced by the emperor reclaimed wastelands for the cultivation of crops.

Along the south bank of the Wei River near Hsien-yang the emperor erected a new and splendid capital city. So that his new metropolis would be inhabited by the educated elite, and in order to destroy the feudal power of the landed aristocracy, he transported some 120,000 wealthy people from all parts of the empire to Hsien-yang. Nothing remains today of more than two hundred elaborate palaces that lined the main streets of the city, for they were looted and burned by Han dynasty troops after the emperor's death.

Ch'in Shih Huang's military government was progressive but it was also ruthless. The emperor felt that the conservative ideas of Confucius were a threat, so he buried alive 460 Confucian scholars who openly opposed his reforms. Then he burned all the books of Confucius except for those in the imperial library. The emperor's eldest son would not go along with his father's action and was sent into exile.

When I visited the Sian Historical Museum, I saw photos of the hill where the books were supposed to have been burned. Beside them hung a portrait of Ch'in Shih Huang dressed in his royal attire—a handsome man, rather portly, with a thin, curved mustache and a tapered beard. I asked one of my Chinese companions why he thought the emperor had done what he did. His reply revealed the attitude of the Chinese today toward Confucians. "The Confucians," he said, "believed that the old ways were too sacred to be changed. They always go back to the writings of Confucius. How can progress be made if nothing can be changed? If Confucian scholars obstructed all reforms, we would remain in the feudal society with old ideas and customs that oppress the people forever."

Largely because of the book burnings and the emperor's abusive use of manpower, most historians of China have regarded him as a villain. And yet, as Edward Thomas Williams, the late American historian, points out in *A Short History of China*, "Nothing more clearly reveals the status of the common man in the ancient world than the practice among all nations of moving vast populations from one area to another without ever consulting their desires in regard to the matter," adding that all ancient emperors used forced labor to build their tombs. Other modern historians, such as C. P. Fitzgerald, stress Ch'in Shih Huang's improvements in communications and food production as well as the endurance of the emperor's administrative structure, which became the basis of government in all subsequent dynasties.

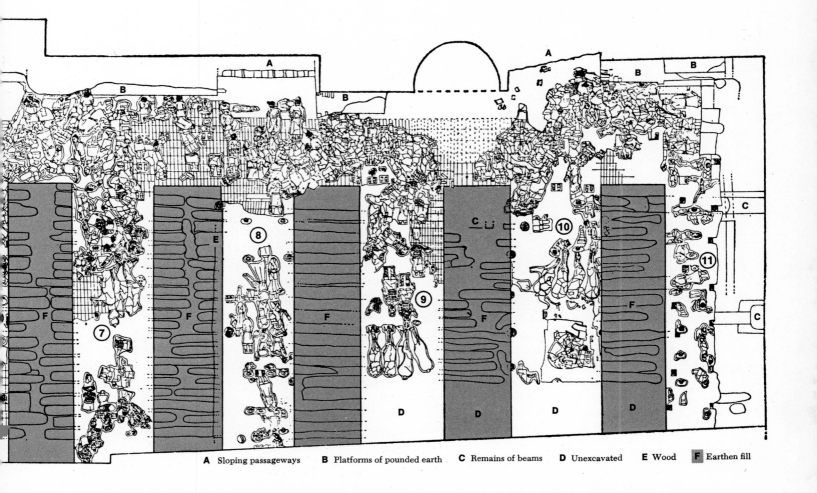

A Sloping passageways   **B** Platforms of pounded earth   **C** Remains of beams   **D** Unexcavated   **E** Wood   **F** Earthen fill

Pottery horses found in the vault were once harnessed four abreast (top) to wooden chariots now mostly destroyed. Some of the soldiers and horses were cleaned (above, middle) and put on view at the Sian Museum. Their striking features, and the spirited expressions of the horses (above) have led scholars to reappraise the beginnings of realism in Chinese art, hitherto attributed to the later Han dynasty. Now archaeologists are raising the question: did the sculptors of the emperor Ch'in's army invent this dramatic style, or will some equally vivid works be unearthed one day in an even earlier tomb?

In spite of the emperor's power and success, he lived a life of fear and secrecy. He traveled almost compulsively, sometimes disguising himself as a peasant and walking the streets of strange cities to find out what people thought of him. He was so terrified of assassination that in his later years he changed his sleeping quarters every night, as his astrologers advised. The palaces were all fully furnished, supplied at all times with servants, concubines, and food, so all would be ready for him at any time and no one need know where he slept. Any person who revealed his whereabouts was immediately put to death along with his entire family.

He was also prey to gross superstitions. Charlatans and practitioners of the occult enriched themselves by exploiting his credulity. Williams tells a story from the *Shih Chi* (or *Historical Record*) of Ssŭ-ma Ch'ien about the emperor and a "fountain of youth." Magicians had told him of three islands in the Eastern Seas where old age and death were unknown because the people who lived there had discovered the "elixir of immortality." Determined to have it himself, the aging emperor sent a fleet of vessels loaded with precious gifts in search of the "Islands of Immortals." After some time the captain of the fleet returned to say he had found the islands and met one of the immortals, who had refused to give him the elixir because his gifts were too cheap. "What gifts do you desire?" asked the captain. "Young men and maidens and craftsmen of all sorts," replied the immortal. So the captain set off again with three thousand of Ch'in's finest young people. They sailed away and never returned. Some historians think they colonized Japan, and, indeed, today there is an ancient coastal town in eastern Japan called Ch'in Shih Huang Ti.

His life was so secret that when he died during a journey to the eastern provinces, no one in the imperial cortege knew it except for his chief eunuch, Chao Kao, and the prime minister, Li Ssŭ, who preferred to keep it a secret for their own reasons. The dying emperor had appointed his exiled eldest son, Fusu, as emperor, but Chao Kao feared that his power would end under Fusu. Instead he and Li Ssŭ sent a forged letter to Fusu ordering him to commit suicide. He obeyed.

While they schemed to enthrone the youngest son, Huhai, whom they could control, the procession traveled the hundreds of miles back to Hsien-yang with the dead emperor's body. In the heat of the summer the chief eunuch and prime minister were obliged to put some rancid fish on a cart following the imperial carriage to hide the odor of the decomposing corpse.

After Huhai succeeded to the throne in 210 B.C., Ch'in Shih Huang's putrifying body was at last laid to rest in a magnificent sarcophagus that was buried with full pomp in the splendid subterranean palace the emperor had spent so many years constructing. Ssŭ-ma Ch'ien relates that after the faithful pallbearers had placed the casket in the sepulchral chamber and were arranging the funerary furniture on their way out, Huhai ordered the great stone door of the tomb closed and sealed, and traps set to protect the entrance against intruders. The pallbearers, the only ones that could reveal the entrance to the

Ch'in Shih Huang

Ch'in Shih Huang was the first emperor of China. A tyrant, he is said to have buried 460 Confucian scholars alive and burned their books, right, but his many achievements include a uniform script, in which his name is written, left.

treasure house, were buried alive with the monarch who had decreed that no more people be buried alive, as had been the custom in some feudal states. Ch'in Shih Huang had chosen a pottery army instead of a real one to guard his tomb.

Three years of mourning were declared, but before that time passed, the Ch'in dynasty had collapsed. In a rebellion led by General Hsiang Yu, an aristocrat seeking to restore his power, the emperor Huhai was captured and killed with three hundred royal relatives. The capital was looted and the emperor's elaborate palaces were razed. Then in 202 B.C., in a major peasant revolution, Liu Pang overthrew Hsiang Yu and became the first emperor of the Han dynasty.

During this period of anarchy, according to Mr. Chen Hsueh-hua, an archaeologist at the Ch'in tomb site, the underground army was found by Hsiang Yu's men because the earth covering it was still rough and discolored. The soldiers were apparently in a hurry because they only smashed a small percentage of the figures and stole some of the weapons before they set fire to the building that had been constructed over the underground vault. The building, the support beams of the underground structure, and the chariots were destroyed; the

The emperor Ch'in built the Great Wall, beginning in 214 B.C., to keep out invaders.

earth sank over the remains of the unique legions and vegetation soon covered the site.

The position of the pottery army about four thousand feet east of the emperor's tomb mound leads to speculation that in keeping with the Chinese theory of yin and yang and traditional ideas of symmetrical balance, an equally spectacular treasure house lies buried an equal distance west of the tomb—perhaps containing statues of officials, ministers, and ladies of the imperial court. Then there is the tomb itself, where the emperor's sarcophagus and unknown treasures lie in a subterranean palace beneath a giant tumulus sometimes called Mount Li. It stands unpretentiously in the middle of a millet field, an odd-looking symmetrical hill. Pine trees cover its original three terraces, symbolic of the harmonious cosmos made up of hell, earth, and heaven. In the surrounding fields peasants go about their plowing as usual, seemingly unconcerned that their water buffaloes and tractors are plowing up the once sacred land that still holds perhaps the richest treasures in the history of China.

Mr. Chen Hsueh-hua, who came with us from the dig, explained that the tumulus was originally built in the center of an enclosed area containing sacred stone tablets, inscribed soul towers, prayer temples, and other symbolic edifices. This was encompassed by a square-walled "inner city." A wide moat then enclosed the entire "spirit city," which had a circumference of 3.5 miles and a total area of 150 acres. Some rocky mounds are all that remain of the walls and temples, and the sacred objects that were placed aboveground have long since been carried away by invading armies. But the earth mound still protects and guards the inner sanctuary.

The tomb is marked by a single stone tablet at the western base that reveals nothing of the inner glories described in Ssŭ-ma Ch'ien's annals. According to these, as reported by Williams in *A Short History of China*, the earth was excavated down to the water springs and a floor of bronze was put in. On this a miniature representation of Ch'in Shih Huang's newly united empire was inlaid with jade and other precious jewels.

"I only hope that I live to see it"

By JOSEPH NEEDHAM

A world-famous historian of Chinese science assesses for HORIZON *the meaning of the new discovery and what may be yet to come.*

There can be no doubt that one of the greatest turning points of all Chinese history was the success of Ch'in Shih Huang Ti ("the imperial ruler of the house of Ch'in"), in the third century B.C., in uniting the whole of China into a single unified state or empire. He laid the foundation of that great, bureaucratic agrarian culture that lasted for two thousand years. So earthshaking was his rise to power and so great the power he wielded that a wealth of legends grew up about him and his times, and we are still sorting out these stories.

It seems that rather too much has been said about Ch'in Shih Huang's draconian authoritarianism. On the contrary, he probably generated a great enthusiasm among the people for a unified state; hence the success of his conquering armies. The people must have been utterly tired of the individual, contending feudal states, and they would have welcomed definitive laws that made no distinction between rich and poor, aristocrat and commoner. Improvements such as the standardization of the written script and of weights and measures and even the regulation of cartwheel gauges must also have been popular.

Just as the unification of the empire was perhaps the greatest event in Chinese history, so also these new discoveries are an outstanding success for contemporary Chinese archaeology. There are several points to be made about them. First, the fact that they are there at all indicates that Chinese culture was advanced enough by then to bury pottery figures instead of immolating thousands of living soldiers, guards, and servants. Eight hundred years earlier the Chinese rulers had not been so humane, for in the royal tombs of the Shang dynasty the skeletons of many sacrificed charioteers and concubines have been found.

Perhaps the greatest interest of the subterranean army of pottery figures rests in the light that they will throw on the history of military technology. Many weapons of bronze have been found, perhaps of iron also, the analyses of which will be important. The forms of the helmets are interesting, for we know that as far back as the Shang, helmets were being made of bronze, and a few have survived. The history of armor in China did not take the same course as in the Western world; it always remained plate armor, as we see in these pictures (page 7), and it was often made of rhinoceros hide. Even paper was used. As is generally known, paper was a Chinese invention, usually ascribed to the Han dynasty, which followed the Ch'in, but it might have been as early as Ch'in Shih Huang's time. And believe it or not, it is possible to make a kind of papier-mâché so hard as to resist the impact of arrows and sword blades.

Among the most interesting things to look out for in Ch'in Shih Huang's subterranean army will be the crossbows, for their triggers of bronze are among the finest mechanical engineering designs and metallurgic foundrywork in any ancient civilization. The harness on the horses, too, will be of major importance, for China had a priority of eight centuries in the development of the breast-strap harness for horses and some seven centuries in the development of the collar harness.

It is indeed possible that three more of these underground brigades of praetorian guards will be found, that is, to the south, the west, and the north of the tumulus of the first emperor. I only hope that I live to see such discoveries and, perhaps even more, the investigation of the contents of the tumulus itself. I know this tumulus quite well; it lies to the east of Lin-t'ung and is so big that it seems like a natural hill. I have gathered the wildflowers, especially a beautiful kind of pink, that grow on it. Ssŭ-ma Ch'ien, the first and greatest historian of China, describes in his *Shih Chi*, finished about 90 B.C., the relief map with the rivers of mercury that was placed in it and the robot crossbow men that were installed to defend the entrances.

Everyone should pay a tribute, not only to the brilliant archaeological scholars of contemporary China, but also to those peasants drilling for water, who knew they had discovered something tremendous and hastened to report it.

The courses of the Yangtze and the Yellow rivers with their tributaries, which the emperor linked by a series of canals, were marked by channels of liquid mercury. The ceiling of the great tomb glowed with the constellations, the North Star, symbol of the Ch'in dynasty, at the center. Lamps with an infinite supply of slow-burning oil were to provide eternal light for the emperor who thought he ruled the world in life and would symbolically rule the universe in death.

The old writings reveal that the concealed entrance was guarded by hidden booby traps: weapons arranged to destroy any and all who might venture to trespass. The emperor's tombs were held sacred, and fear of arousing the wrath of the evil spirits who protected the dead kept the grave robbers— who stole ruthlessly from tombs of less important people— away from the imperial tombs.

Now the People's Republic of China has become the first government of China to systematically and scientifically excavate, restore, and preserve the ancient tombs—not for financial gain, but to educate the Chinese about their heritage. The Chinese peasants, inspired by Mao Tse-tung's words "Let the past serve the present," are eager to help. As more wells are being sunk and more land leveled in preparation for complete mechanization of farming by 1980, they are constantly finding relics that lead to new discoveries. Beneath the earth in one of the world's oldest civilization, there are still hundreds of imperial, military, and other tombs to be excavated.

The People's Republic of China has allocated substantial resources for archaeological projects and the restoration of temples, pagodas, monasteries, gates and walls, Buddhist temple-caves, and other historical monuments. Twenty-one of the fifty-three Yunkang temple-caves in Datung and the spectacular Dragon Gate caves near the old capital of Lo-yang, both from the fifth and sixth centuries B.C., have been restored and are already open to the public. The history of China is unfolding in these restorations and archaeological finds. The period of China's first emperor, Ch'in Shih Huang, is perhaps the most fascinating of all, and we will surely learn more about it in the excavations still to come. □

In the vault the careful work of excavation proceeds

How to Think about Politicians

The ground rule is to be wary of what they say and observe what they do.
Take Woodrow Wilson, for example . . .

For the past two years I have been engaged in a study of how and why America entered certain of her foreign wars. The chief fruit of that inquiry is the conviction that we are fast losing our capacity to think politically, to think, that is, in the same mode as the great historians from Thucydides to Mommsen, to think as Machiavelli thought, as the authors of *The Federalist Papers* thought, as Abraham Lincoln thought.

Wilson campaigns in 1912, left; Lyndon Johnson, right, faces the press in 1967. Both denounced war and then pursued war policies.

What political thinking means is best illustrated by an example of its absence. Many historians have described in great detail how America became involved in the First World War. A number of critical scholars (including Charles Tansill, a disciple of the great historian Charles Beard) have shown convincingly that during our "neutral" period President Wilson pursued a diplomatic course that was grossly partial to the Allies and hostile to Germany. Wilson's diplomacy, they have also shown, was based largely on the assertion of certain rights of neutrality whose existence was dubious in international law, whose practical value was nil, whose adoption set the United States quite needlessly on a collision course with Germany. However, it has occurred to none of these critical scholars that Wilson charted that diplomatic course because he *wanted* to bring America into the European war. Quite the contrary. These critics of Wilson's diplomacy insist that he hoped to avoid war. For them, Wilson's diplomacy was one thing, Wilson another.

No failure of political thinking can be much more glaring than this, because it violates the first and most important rule of reasonable thought: that people must be regarded as intending the obvious consequences of their actions. The rule is neither novel nor recondite nor arbitrary. It is a maxim we apply all the time in our personal dealings; if we did not we would meet with disaster soon enough. It is also a fundamental maxim of the law; if we did not apply it in court, law itself would disappear. In court a defendant who really did not intend the consequences of his act is rightly regarded as mad; he is put in an asylum instead of a prison. But when it comes to politics, we tend to regard our elected leaders as intending almost anything but the consequences of their deeds.

An example from congressional politics illustrates the point. Every two years for decades Democratic legislators have met in secret caucus before the start of each new Congress and voted in favor of

people, rules, and procedures that confer upon a small minority of conservative Democrats the lion's share of legislative power. In other words, a large number of ostensibly liberal Democrats regularly bestow upon people opposed to their liberal programs the power to defeat or decimate them. We believe—having been told —that the disproportionate power of conservative Democrats in Congress is due to an all-powerful dispensation known as the "seniority system." In fact, that "system" is no more than the procedure agreed upon by Democrats to produce the intended result. Never ascribe to a "system" what is due to the people who operate it—that is why Machiavelli talked about "The Prince" when he wrote about politics. By that device he took politics out of the realm of medieval abstractions and returned it to its proper place—the actions of men.

In part the flight from intention—the heart of political thinking—is the result of our credulity. Public people are often regarded as not intending the consequences of their actions because they explicitly disavow the intention. Wilson constantly deplored war. Consequently he could not have wanted to see Americans fighting in France. President McKinley deplored imperialism. Consequently, though he planned to seize and did seize the Philippine Islands as an American colony, he is still taken at his own word, namely that he did what he did because, alas, he had no alternative.

By WALTER KARP

President Lyndon Johnson said he wanted "no wider war" in Asia; he was forced step by step into the "quagmire" as the result of an inexorable "decision-making process." Political thinking deals with such explanations by another simple and universal maxim: "Actions speak louder than words." Political thinking demands that we judge the words of rulers by their actions, rather than their actions by their words.

Behind such credulity lies our modern reluctance to admit the potency of political ambition as a primary fact of life. To deliberately bring a nation into a titanic, faraway war, to willfully rupture a republic's traditions by founding an imperial regime imply that political ambition is far more grand, far more consequential, far more terrible than we care to recognize. We prefer to think of political ambition as a paltry and derivative passion, of little force compared to the ambition to amass a huge fortune. We find it easier to imagine a billionaire wanting a war in order to gain millions of dollars than to concede that a ruler might want to wage war in order to gain everlasting glory. To evade the terror and the grandeur of political ambition, scholars give credence to pious disavowals and espouse the modern doctrine (an invention of the titanic genius of Karl Marx) that rulers do not matter at all, that they are the pawns of social forces and processes, that their ambitions, actions, and intentions are only flotsam on the swift-flowing river of history.

Political thinking does not deal in the abstract. Its rule is that when we look at history we examine what actually happened—not forces and processes but people and their myriad actions. "I frame no hypotheses," said the great Newton, and so it is with political thinking. Dealing with the actual deeds of men, political thinking requires us to frame no hypothetical forces to "explain" them. We do not assume in advance that rulers always act under the compulsion of a mere theoretical necessity. Necessity, as William Pitt once remarked, is "the argument of tyrants [and] the creed of slaves."

The critics of Wilson's diplomacy have generally attributed it not to Wilson but to insuperable economic forces, pressures, and interests. What actually happened is quite different. Nobody on Wall Street "forced" Wilson or even dared to suggest that he take the stand he took against Germany. Wilson had charted his course, Wall Street interests saw profit in supporting it, but the initiative was entirely Wilson's. He acted first. Involved here is another important rule of political thinking. To think politically means to think chronologically. It means distinguishing between earlier and later, between what came first and what came second. The oldtime schoolteachers who drilled dates into children's heads may have been dreary instructors, but they had the heart of political thinking within them. Trends are created by rulers. Powerful rulers initiate powerful trends.

By dealing with events in the order of their occurrence, by eschewing abstract forces and necessities, by grasping deeds and inferring intentions, political thinking recovers the reality of political power and hence the reality, the importance, the grandeur, and the terror of political ambition itself. There is nothing mysterious about political power. From whatever source it may be derived, it means, quite simply, the capacity to act and so make a difference in the common and public world. It is the capacity, as the political philosopher Hannah Arendt put it, "to make a new beginning." People seek that capacity for a variety of reasons: because they love distinction, as John Adams insisted; because they wish to win fame and glory; because they wish to help their countrymen; because they wish to lord it over them; because they wish far more than others do to matter. Men have rarely sought great power for trivial reasons. As Aristotle long ago put it, no one aspires to become a tyrant in order to keep warm.

Recent American presidents have garnered to themselves enormous increments of personal power, yet few among us are left to say openly and frankly that they did so because, like so many rulers before them, they wished to exercise power beyond the law's bounds. The Founding Fathers warned their countrymen again and again of the strength and the dangers of political ambition. Now, two centuries later, we are eager to accept any comforting reason for political deeds except the political ambitions of the doers. That eagerness betrays, I believe, both a loss of courage and a fading of love: the old courage to face political reality; the old love of the "public thing," *res publica*, our Republic. We are more ripe for tyranny than we realize.

As for the intentions of Woodrow Wilson, they would not have puzzled the Founders for a moment. As soon as war broke out in Europe, Woodrow Wilson was fired by a truly grandiose ambition: to preside over the ultimate peace settlement and establish through a league of nations the foundation of "permanent peace." As Wilson's friend Colonel House said to the president in November, 1914, what lay before him was "the noblest part that has ever come to a son of man." That ambition some may deem sublime and others vainglorious, but such was the president's ambition, and there was no way to achieve it except by entering the war. As Wilson himself told Jane Addams on the eve of our entry, he would have no influence at the peace conference if America remained neutral. At best, the belligerents would let him "call through a crack in the door."

For half a century Wilson's admirers have lauded his sublime and driving ambition, and Wilson's critics have shown that his diplomacy led needlessly to war. No one fit together an ambition that required war and a diplomacy that invited it. I know of no better example of the failure to think politically.

One thing more: Political thinking may not shape our formal discourse or make itself heard in our political discussions, but perhaps we understand more than we say. In the nation's capital, a city of monuments and memorials, there stands not a single notable monument to President Woodrow Wilson. ☐

Secrets of Anamorphic Art

Out of the past and into a new exhibition comes a forgotten visual game

By SUSAN FERRIS

Namorphicay rtay. That's pig Latin for anamorphic art. Pig Latin is a children's word game. To play, take a normal word, chop off the first letter, affix it to the end, and add -*y* or -*ay*. The new word sounds like gibberish, but those who know the trick can easily figure out what is being said.

Anamorphic art is pig Latin in pictures. To play, an artist takes an image and drastically distorts it according to a set of complex rules. The swirl of color or blur of black and white that results is difficult—sometimes impossible—to make sense of. Unless you know the trick. View the picture from a certain oblique angle, or examine its reflection in a cylindrical, conical, or pyramidal mirror placed on a particular spot in the composition, and magically the swirls and blurs come together into the original, conventional shape. As the Greek etymology suggests, the form (*morphē*) emerges again (*ana*). Hence the name of the game.

Players have run the gamut from master painters of the Italian Renaissance and political satirists of sixteenth-century Germany to erotic artists of Georgian England and toy manufacturers of nineteenth-century America. In our own era the French art historian Jurgis Baltrušaitis devoted a volume to

The face in the anamorphoscope: Portrait of Louis XIII, *by Jean-François Niceron, is merely a swirl of color until it is viewed in a cylindrical mirror, which reveals His Majesty's disdainful smile and chilling gaze.*

anamorphic art, and a few artists, including Salvador Dali, tried their hands at it. But anamorphosis has been largely forgotten, and surviving specimens have been neglected or relegated, as optical diversions, to museums of natural history.

Recently, however, a young Dutchman, Joost Elffers, happened upon an anamorphosis in a junk shop, and his curiosity was aroused. Elffers shared his find with another Dutchman, photographer Michael Schuyt, and together they dreamed up a traveling show of anamorphoses. The two persuaded a bank to finance further research, then

Museumgoers in Amsterdam admiring anamorphic art

On display: "Anamorphoses: Games of Perception and Illusion in Art," an exhibition of more than one hundred anamorphic works, is now touring American museums, as follows:
- Brooklyn Museum, New York, December 17, 1976–February 13, 1977
- Cleveland Museum of Art, March 30–May 15
- Museum of Science and Industry, Chicago, June 15–September 8
- Corcoran Gallery of Art, Washington, D.C., October 20–January 15, 1978
- High Museum of Art, Atlanta, March 1–May 1

The exhibition was brought to the United States by means of a grant from SCM Corporation. The illustrations accompanying this article were selected from *Hidden Images: Games of Perception, Anamorphic Art, Illusion* by Michael Schuyt and Joost Elffers, recently published by Harry N. Abrams, Inc.

More than meets the eye: *Leonardo da Vinci's sketch of a child's face, above, is hardly up to standard. Yet from the side, the elongated features appear normal; drawn about 1485, this is one of the first known anamorphoses. Erhard Shön, a follower of Albrecht Dürer, applied the technique in the woodcut opposite, about 1535. View it aslant from the bound edge of this page with one eye shut, and four faces will emerge. Hans Holbein's portrait* The Ambassadors, *left, painted in 1533, conceals a grim reminder of our mortality. The anamorphic blur at the base, seen slantwise, is the skull below.*

began looking for more examples of this illusive art. By 1975 they had their exhibition. It opened in Amsterdam that fall, then in Paris the next winter, in Boston last September, and is currently installed at the Brooklyn Museum in New York. This year and next it will travel across the United States and to Japan. By 1979 anamorphic art will undoubtedly be, as one critic has predicted, "one of the best-known obscurities in the history of art."

The earliest known examples of anamorphic art come to us from a page in Leonardo da Vinci's notebooks. Preserved in *Codex Atlanticus* are two hesitant scribbles—one resembling a baby's face, the other a human eye. From the front the face and eye look oddly elongated. But when viewed from a certain point on the right side, just above the surface of the paper, the figures take on normal proportions. They also seem to disengage from the paper and float into the air. Leonardo sketched these about 1485, probably because he, like other Renaissance artists, was seeking alternatives to central perspective.

His investigations were tentative at best, but in the next two centuries the methods of constructing anamorphoses were perfected. In one technique the artist drew a normal representation of an object on paper, perforated the paper along the lines of the drawing, placed it at right angles to the wall where the anamorphic image was to be painted, and directed light through the holes onto the wall. This produced an elongated image, which he then traced and painted. Seen from the point where the light had originated, the distorted painting appeared normal. In another technique the artist sketched an image,

The anamorphic eye: *The distorted sign marking a Dutch bicycle path, above right, looks normal to the passing cyclist. At right, in a 1646 engraving, an artist makes an anamorphic fresco by dividing a picture into squares, stretching strings to the wall, and (if not hopelessly confused) transferring the contents of each square in distorted form to the corresponding section of the wall.*

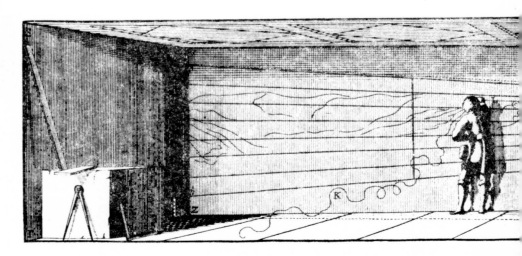

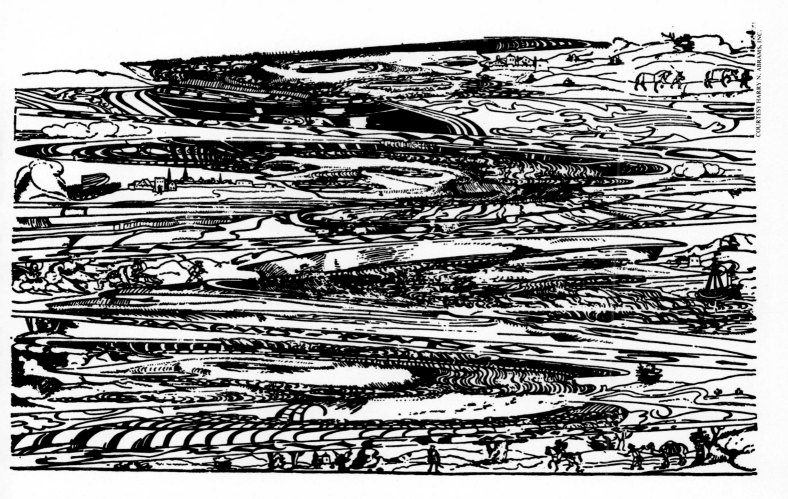

overlaid it with a grid, resketched each square in the corresponding unit of a geometrically distorted matrix, then filled in each of the units to produce the final image.

The methods were cumbersome, but by mastering them, a painter could not only, as a seventeenth-century treatise points out, avoid "embarrassment when he must paint an oblique-angled, round, or otherwise unusually formed building or vault"; he could also dabble in theatrics. Through anamorphosis an artist might render a subject unrecognizable, then make it reappear with its *trompe-l'oeil* qualities enhanced. Religious

painters employed these properties to simulate miracles: suddenly out of a mysterious amalgam of billowing shapes the figure of Christ would rise. Other artists used these tricks to conceal and then reveal with greater effect a forbidden political, pornographic, or scatological reference.

In the most famous example of anamorphosis, Hans Holbein's *The Ambassadors* (1533), the artist used the technique to belie the meaning of the painting. Two splendidly bedecked diplomats stand beside shelves filled with musical and mathematical instruments. The dual portrait is a testimonial to the

worldly accomplishments of its subjects, but for one unexplained image—a curious white blur near the base of the picture. That blur is an anamorphic conceit. Viewed from an angle near the right edge of the frame, it becomes a skull—a secret reminder of the transience of life and the relativity of material success. This grim little joke from the painter may also be a rebus, or pictorial pun, on his name, which does, in fact, mean "skull": *hohle Bein* is hollow bone.

In the 1600's anamorphic art flourished and new types proliferated. The Dutch introduced the *perspectyfka*,

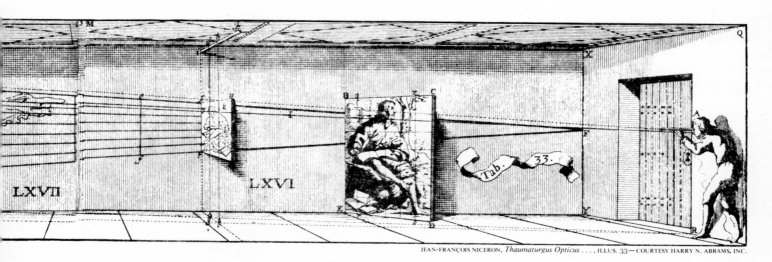

Icons for three eras: *For the present day, what else but the Coca-Cola can, above anamorphosized by a Dutch artist, Hans Hamngren, and resolved at left? From the eighteenth century comes the handsome man-of-war below, Lord Nelson's flagship, H.M.S. Victory, in a work attributed to James Steer. Opposite is a raising of the Cross that was painted in the seventeenth century by a follower of Peter Paul Rubens.*

Face-lift: *Henry Kettle, a leading anamorphic artist in Georgian England, apparently had the instinct of a plastic surgeon. His painting from about 1770,* Four Male Portraits Become One, *above, exhibits four misshapen countenances. However, when sorted out by a reflecting pyramid, the best features of each face combine to produce a fifth, almost prepossessing, portrait, right center.*

or perspective cabinet—a box featuring a distorted picture on the back that looked normal when viewed through a spyhole on the front. Anamorphoses that could be read only with the aid of reflecting cylinders, and cones and pyramids as well, came into vogue. In 1638 the most important treatise on anamorphic technique was published—Jean-Francois Niceron's *La Perspective curieuse*. Niceron, a painter, mathematician, and monk, lived in a monastery off the Place Royale in Paris. Descartes, too, lived there for a time, and it is thought that Niceron's interest in the optical aspects of illusion and reality may have aroused Descartes's interest in metaphysics.

As soon as the challenges of anamorphic type, technique, and meaning had been met, the great experimenters retreated, leaving the form to its popularizers. In the 1700's countless series of anamorphic engravings were sold, and a machine was invented for the construction of anamorphoses. In the 1800's anamorphic games were manufactured. The genre receded into the playroom

then and by the twentieth century had all but disappeared.

Modern artists and art historians have tended to dismiss anamorphic art as mere gimmickry. Why then has it suddenly attracted such a following—drawing 250,000 visitors in Amsterdam and Paris alone?

For one thing, anamorphic art is fun. It affords the opportunity of making sense out of nonsense, of making the unintelligible instantly intelligible. That is hardly a common occurrence in life or —especially these days—in art.

The attraction of anamorphic art may also stem from a reaction against the

hermetic tendencies in modern painting. While the meaning of abstract expressionist, minimal, or conceptual works may be clear to painters and critics, it often eludes museumgoers. Not so with anamorphoses. Here, for once, the viewer can make abstractions yield conventional images. His role in interpreting the art is crucial—and that is indeed a pleasant change.

Unlike most of the serious painting of our day, anamorphoses aim to involve, amuse, and flatter their audience. Perhaps this minor genre is getting major play because it contains more than one hidden message. □

Good housekeeping: *The curious—almost cubistic—anamorphic painting, right, of a cluttered hall with a tilted floor and crooked columns covers the inside panels of a perspective cabinet made, possibly by Samuel Van Hoogstraten, in Holland in 1663. Disorder —just this once—in a Dutch interior? Not at all. Look through the peephole, left, on the front of the cabinet, and all the elements fall tidily into place.*

MEMENTO MORI

Takeoff for Disaster

How the plan for a fleet of
imperial airships came to grief with R101,
the biggest and most expensive
flying machine the world had ever seen

At once exhausted and inspired by their experiences in the First World War, the British of the 1920's set about to revive that pride and emblem of their glories, the empire. It had been acquired, according to a famous phrase, "in a fit of absence of mind," and not for the first time they resolved to give it a firmer sense of order. They explored the idea of federal unity for all its constituent parts. They dreamed of an empire free trade area. They mounted the vast exhibition in Wembley in 1924 to rekindle the imperial passions among a war-weary public. They sought means, as always, of binding the empire more tightly, making its separate territories more familiar with one another, speeding the traffic between them, and so ensuring that Sydney and New Delhi, Ottawa and Cape Town, remained as truly British as London itself.

To this end they devised a scheme to link the greater possessions of the empire by the thrilling new medium of the air—an imperial air service, an all-red route through the skies, "giving a grand new meaning," as one of its proponents declared, "to this imperishable empire of ours."

• • •

Technique was always the key to empire. Supremacy of technique had enabled the British to impose their will on India and Africa in the first place, and technique had held together the ramshackle imperial structure ever since. In techniques of communication, especially, the British had been unchallenged throughout the nineteenth century. Sea traffic was overwhelmingly in their hands, and the entire pattern of maritime method and custom had been their creation. Underwater cables were a British specialty, and so were railways, so that the British Empire, scattered haphazardly over all the continents, had been in many ways a pacemaker in means of movement and converse. Every empire depends upon its communications, but the British more than any: half the imperial energies had been spent on exploring, pioneering, and developing new ways of distributing London's authority among the far-flung dependencies of the crown.

By the 1920's this inventiveness was

Lord Thompson of Cardington, chief promoter of the R101. Opposite: a stream of ballast water is released from the airship during a test run, 1929.

flagging, and the imperial confidence had weakened with it. Rival industrial powers had arisen to defy the pre-eminence of the British and make them feel less providentially masters of their fate. Britain was no longer the world's workshop, as it had been in the heady generations after the Industrial Revolution. In 1912 the sinking on her maiden voyage of the *Titanic*, the greatest liner ever built, had symbolized the passing of British supremacy in traditional skills, and the superiority of German warships at the Battle of Jutland four years later had confirmed it—"There's something wrong," said Admiral Beatty, watching his vessels explode around him, "with my bloody ships today."

In many newer aspects of technology, too, Britain had been overtaken: in chemistry, in metallurgy, in motor engineering. The Admiralty failed to make international radio as British an institution as the cables had been, and the great British railway engineers moved reluctantly out of their beloved steam and into diesel and electric traction. So it was with more optimism than assurance, perhaps, that the imperialists now turned to the most obvious element for new imperial enterprises, the air. Though they possessed, at the end of the war, easily the largest air force in the world, in many ways they were still behind their rivals technically.

Boldly, nevertheless, almost the moment the armistice was signed, enthusiasts began to think about an imperial air service. This could revolutionize the very nature of the empire, as the advent of steamships had in the previous century. The idea that the king-emperor might be in London one week, Canberra or Vancouver the next, seemed to give the whole imperial concept a new dimension. Fortunately there was already on hand an instrument awesome enough to match the grandeur of the vision: not the noisy, waspish, and inelegant airplane, but the rigid airship, one of the stateliest expressions of technique yet devised by man. Few people thought the airplane could ever master the vast distances of the empire routes, but the airship could. It could be both a means and a symbol of imperial revival.

In 1924, then, the government of the day, under Ramsay MacDonald, officially adopted the Imperial Airship Scheme, intended to provide a regular passenger service along the principal route of the British Empire, the route to India. This, though, would be only the beginning: one day flotillas of those great vehicles would be serenely sailing through all the imperial skies, saluting each other as they passed over Suez or magnificently perceived in the dawn light of mid-Atlantic.

• • •

The airship was *not* a British specialty. Though the English had been early

The R 101, partially assembled, above, was built in an oversize hangar at Cardington, Bedfordshire. Within the steel framework, one of the seventeen gasbags that would lift the airship is being test-inflated.

into the air by balloon and had pioneered long flights in heavier-than-air machines, they had neglected the rigid dirigible—the steerable airship, that is, with huge gasbags contained within a fabric-covered framework. This was essentially a German product. Since 1900 Count Ferdinand von Zeppelin, the genius of German airships, had been steadily improving and developing his designs, and during the war his aircraft had done prodigious things. They had frequently raided London and reconnoitered the English coast, and sometimes they made far longer flights: one zeppelin had flown

from Germany to east Africa to drop supplies to be beleaguered German forces there. The zeppelins had reached heights of more than twenty thousand feet and had proved themselves safe and reliable.

All the recent British airships had been direct copies of zeppelins. One of them, the R34, had flown the Atlantic in 1919, the first airship to do so, and the first aircraft of any kind to make the double crossing. Otherwise the British record had hardly been encouraging. One airship fell apart. One flew into a hill. One broke up in midair on a trial flight. The cadre of British airship men was very small indeed: a mere handful of fliers, mostly from the Royal Air Force and Royal Navy, backed by a few eager scientists and engineers. They copied German methods almost slavishly—including, it was said, the mistakes.

But the Imperial Airship Scheme envisaged altogether new airships of entirely British design. By modern standards the technology was hardly sophisticated. Even the Germans worked to fairly rough standards, and any airship of the period was a much more primitive vehicle than, say, an ocean liner. The bags containing the lifting gas, for example, were made of goldbeater's skin—membranes from bullocks' intestines. The outer fabric was generally of silk, the structural framework of wood or aluminum. Sights were

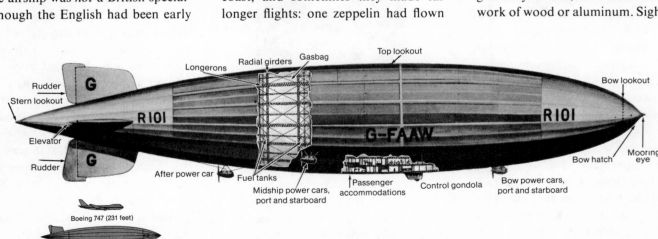

The completed R 101, in the diagram above, was 131 feet in diameter and 777 feet long—more than three times longer than today's biggest aircraft, the Boeing 747, but still considerably shorter than a supertanker.
DIAGRAM: CAL SACKS

taken on most airships of the day by a man standing in an open cockpit high on top of the airship; sometimes he would find himself, all alone up there, skimming through the top of a cloud, his head in open sky, the great form of the airship beneath him hidden in swirling vapor.

More than once, when the Germans were lost in the clouds over England, they lowered a man on a rope into clear air to find out where they were, and on the ground it took hundreds of men with ropes to manhandle an airship out of its hangar. Airship engines, generally mounted in pods beneath the craft, were terribly noisy and smelly and could be reached only by open ladders. Accommodation was usually very limited, either in a gondola slung beneath the airship or in compartments built within the envelope itself. The airship was really an astonishingly inefficient machine, too. A vehicle as long as an ocean liner could lift hardly more than a truckload, and an absurdly small proportion of its bulk could be put to any useful purpose at all.

Still, some British airship men had great faith in the machine, and their enthusiasm was infectious. MacDonald's was Britain's first Socialist government, and so it was decreed that the two first empire airships would have ideological as well as imperial meaning. One, codenamed R100 (*R* for "rigid") was to be built by a private company at Howden, in Yorkshire. The other, R101, would be built by the government itself. Specifications would be the same for both, but the Labour ministers clearly hoped that the state enterprise would make a better showing than the capitalist, and the air minister, a retired army officer named Christopher Thomson, threw all his influence and enthusiasm behind the R101. The Air Ministry undertook an elaborate program of research, and £1 million was earmarked for development.

The R101 was to be built at Cardington, the Royal Airship Works near Bedford, which would later become the home base of the imperial airship service. The airship shed there was enlarged, making it the biggest building in the British Empire, and a twin was built beside it, to house the R100 when the time came. There the design team, it was said, "lived and worked like a religious community intent upon their single purpose"; and so proud was Thomson himself of the project, so confident of its significance, that when he was elevated to the peerage that year, he took the name of the airship works for his title and became Lord Thomson of Cardington.

. . .

Cardington still stands and is still an RAF station. Its sheds are no longer the largest structures under the crown, but they still look enormous, and from almost anywhere in the flattish, dullish country round about seem to dominate the landscape almost primevally—eerily, too, for from a distance they look like a pair of gigantic burial mounds.

There the dedicated design team spent six years building the R101. It was the biggest and most expensive flying machine that had ever been devised—more than a million oxen provided intestinal membranes for its seventeen gasbags. Much of it was innovative. There were diesel engines instead of the usual gasoline engines. There was a steel framework instead of wood or aluminum. There were new kinds of valves, new steering motors, new harnesses for the gasbags, new dope for stiffening the fabric. In its final form the R101 was 777 feet long. It was propelled by five engines, slung in pods, and was designed to carry one hundred passengers at speeds up to seventy miles an hour. It was more complex than any previous airship, it was more thoroughly planned, and above all it was bigger. Dr. Hugo Eckener, the zeppelin designer, was once shown the drawings of the R101 and asked his opinion of it. "It is very fine," he answered. "But isn't it a little *big*?"

It was also luxurious. In the old imperial tradition, everything about the R101 was consciously shipshape, as though the imperial airships were in direct line of succession to the British India or P and O liners. Crew and passengers were carried on two decks within the main structure of the airship. The passengers bunked two to a cabin, with dummy portholes to heighten the nautical effect, and the crew wore neonaval uniforms. There was a large dining saloon, ten passengers to a table, and a promenade deck complete with deck chairs and, for viewing the passing earth below, celluloid windows. The passengers' lounge, sixty feet by thirty-two, was embellished with gilded pillars and potted palms. There was a smoking room, too, thoroughly insulated against fire, and a galley with an electric cooking stove and steamer.

To enter the ship one took the elevator to the top of the Cardington mooring tower, which looked rather like the lattice control tower of an American battleship of the period, and, passing through a door in the bow of the vessel, walked along an interior gangway within the skin of the envelope into the living accommodation amidships. The sensation of emerging from that gloomy tunnel into the light and spacious lounge was, so everybody thought, distinctly like boarding a great liner through a hatch in the hull and emerging a few moments later on the sunny boat deck.

The control quarters were on two levels, one within the airship proper, one slung below it, connected by a steel ladder. In the upper cabins the naviga-

Luxury abounded on the R101. Here is the formal dining room.

tor kept his charts and instruments. In the lower were two huge wooden control wheels—one for direction, one for height—the ballast controls, the ship's compass, the engine telegraphs. The wireless room was equipped with the very latest transmitters, with a range of two thousand miles, and a radio telephone that could carry conversations up to a hundred miles. The safety equipment, too, was said to be unprecedented, from auxiliary radios and steering gear to devices that could cut open the fuel tanks and jettison their oil in an emergency.

Along the route to India equally elaborate arrangements were made. Immensely expensive mooring towers were erected at Ismailia, halfway to India, and Karachi, where another gigantic hangar was also built. Weather stations at Malta, Ismailia, Aden, and Baghdad all contributed to a meteorological service more thorough than anything conceived before, and the information was to be collated at a new weather station especially built at Cardington. The R 101, Lord Thomson confidently declared, would be as safe as a house— "except," he cautiously added, "for the millionth chance."

. . .

But if it all sounded solid and modern and comfortable, and if the publicity machine convinced the British public that nothing was being spared to make the R 101 a supreme example of British technology, in fact this was a shaky and specious artifact. There was something amateurish in its construction, something that smacked of compromise and makeshift. The assurance was often bluff. The designers were harassed and hamstrung by political interference. Though it looked an imperial enterprise in the grandest tradition, there was none of the proud certainty, the combination of daring and common sense, that characterized British inventions in the great Victorian days. Many of the Cardington men devel-

oped doubts about the vessel, and their colleagues from Howden viewed the progress of the R 101 with concern.

It was a mistake, perhaps, to think of the airship as a kind of transmuted steamship, for it gave a false sense of security and experience to the whole project. Those gilded pillars in the smoking room looked reassuringly familiar to visitors—"positively an aerial hotel," as one observer reported—but they were not true pillars at all, merely metal struts covered in balsa wood and dressed up with moldings. Those smoking-room armchairs, so clublike in the publicity drawings, were really made only of matchwood. Nothing was quite what it seemed, and so the whole project was spuriously attached to the great tradition.

Technically the airship failed almost from the start to live up to expectations. The engines, designed originally for Canadian railway locomotives, were too heavy and too weak and could not be run at maximum speeds because they vibrated so. The new valves were found to be more ingenious than effective. The new dope for treating the fabric set up a chemical reaction, so that the whole envelope had to be scrapped. During one early flight the airship suddenly plunged into a series of short, staccato dives, so alarming that the first officer on duty refused to fly in it again. Even the galley proved inadequate for the job: when a party of MPs went to Cardington to inspect the airship, the lunch they ate on

board was secretly prepared by RAF cooks on the ground.

In some ways the work was almost too thorough, in others alarmingly makeshift. Hundreds of thousands of pounds were spent on research and experiment, idea after idea was tried and discarded, the design got more and more complicated, the completion date was successively postponed. The Labour government fell, went into opposition, and was re-elected, and still the R 101 was a-building. Up at Howden the R 100 was built to a fixed price, but the Cardington bills went up and up, in afterthought and new estimate, in error and false economy. Yet when it was found that the gasbags were chafing against the steel girders of the ship, causing leaks, wads of padding were simply tied around the protruding metalwork; and far more drastically, when they discovered that the airship's payload would be no more than thirty-five tons, instead of the seventy-seven tons predicted, it was decided to cut the entire airship in half, insert an extra gasbag, and join the structure together again.

Yet enthusiasm still ran high. If one or two men prudently backed out, there was never a shortage of substitutes, while the papers were full of the splendors of it all, providing some measure of national pride through the hangdog days of the depression. The king himself often expressed interest in the work, and the Prince of Wales once drove up to Cardington to see for himself the prodigy growing in its shed.

It was Lord Thomson who conceived a fitting moment for the launching of this, the greatest imperial enterprise of the time. The R 101 made her first trial flight in September, 1929. October, 1930, was the time fixed for the next imperial conference in London, to be attended by the prime ministers of all the self-governing dominions and by representatives of India. As the empire groped toward new purposes, definitions, and constitutional relationships,

Airship 101 passes over London, opposite, on a brief flight in October, 1929. A year later, on October 4, 1930, the captain and some of the passengers on the maiden flight, including Lord Thomson of Cardington (above, second from the right), prepare to go on board.

this meeting might be crucial to the entire future of the organism—might indeed decide whether it would have a future at all. How grand, thought Lord Thomson, who had been tipped as a possible viceroy of India, if the biggest airship on earth could make its maiden voyage along the most imperial of all the imperial routes, to India and back, to bring the air minister himself direct from the frontiers to the conference chamber in Westminster!

So it was arranged. The R 101 would fly from Cardington to Karachi in the autumn of 1930, and on the way it would land beside the Suez Canal, the lifeline of empire, for a celebratory banquet at Ismailia—just as, over so many generations, British battleships had flown the flag and offered hospitality in the imperial ports of call. The towers at Ismailia and Karachi were already built. The weather service was already functioning. The flight could be made in two stages—two nights from England to Egypt, flying spectacularly over the Alps, two nights on to Karachi. Lord Thomson would be accompanied by Sir Sefton Brancker, the director of civil aviation, and the return to London would be scheduled to get him back just in time for the opening of the imperial conference.

Everything at Cardington was now geared to this purpose. The airship had been six years in the building, but now everything was rushed. By September, 1930, it had made only eight flights, all in good weather, all in daylight, none more than thirty hours long. Its engines had never been tested at high speeds. Though a certificate of airworthiness had been issued, it was on the condition that the necessary speed trials should be conducted on the way to India—the test flight, in other words, was to be the maiden voyage itself.

But all the time, as these slipshod preparations continued, as one fault after another was discovered and hastily mended, as the confidence of the crew gradually waned, as it became clear to the Cardington team that they were being rushed into a hazardous venture

—all the time the inexorable light of publicity shone upon the airship. The ballyhoo was enormous, and there was not a child in the kingdom who did not know the name of the R Hundred-and-One. A postponement now, or a failure, would be unthinkable. The R 100 was already successfully flying; the German *Graf Zeppelin* was maintaining a regular service to South America and had once flown around the world. The more eagerly the nation waited for the R 101 to beat them all, the more determined was Lord Thomson that the flight must not be delayed. It took two months to add the airship's new center section, the

In 1924 Prime Minister Ramsay Mac-Donald adopted the airship scheme.

work being completed on October 1, 1930. *Two days* later the R 101 was to leave for India. "They're rushing us," the airship's captain, Flight Lieutenant Carmichael Irwin, told visitors to Cardington that week. "We're not ready, we're just not ready."

. . .

On the evening of October 4, nevertheless, the distinguished passengers arrived at the Royal Airship Works for the great flight. It was a gray, cold night, but as they stepped from their limousines they saw the vast silver shape of the R 101 shining magnificently above their heads. It was ablaze with lights. Searchlights played upon it, and there were rows of bright lights from the passenger quarters and the control cabins, and lights at the top of the mooring mast, and green and red navigation

lights on the fins of the airship. A big crowd had gathered on the airfield, and the lights of hundreds of cars, too, illuminated the whole scene, so that from a distance the massive hulks of the sheds, the resplendent silver shape of the airship at its tower, the crowds milling about the field, the endless stream of headlights pouring along the country roads from Bedford, gave it all an air of fantasy or nightmare.

The crew had been working all day making final preparations and loading the ship, and even now there was a constant clanging up and down the spiral staircase of the tower. Though each crew member was allowed only ten pounds of personal baggage, the passengers were less strictly supervised, and Lord Thomson's luggage included three large cabin trunks. A case of champagne, too, had been loaded for the Ismailia banquet, together with special silver cutlery and potted palms and beer barrels embossed with the crossed flags of Britain and India; and a blue Axminster carpet had been especially laid for the occasion all the length of the entrance corridor and throughout the enormous lounge. To save time refueling at Ismailia and allow more time for ceremonials, an extra supply of diesel fuel was also loaded, so that the airship was heavily overweight.

Fifty-four people boarded the R 101 that evening, the humbler by the tower steps, the grander by its elevator. They were all men. There were twelve passengers, all officials except for Lord Thomson's valet, and forty-two crew, from Irwin, the captain, to J. W. Megginson, the eighteen-year-old galley boy. By six thirty they were all aboard. The crew was at their stations, engineers in the pods, coxswain and captain in the gondola, navigator at his charts, stewards preparing the cabins and dining saloon for dinner, riggers making last-minute checks of gasbags and harnesses. Looking up at the huge shape of the airship, people could see the passengers leaning over the rail on the promenade deck or strolling about the lounge.

The engines took some time to start,

but by six forty-five they had spluttered into life and were thundering at the mooring mast. Slowly the ship backed away, and almost at once her bow dipped slightly, until a vast spray of ballast water, released from the bow, gave her more buoyancy and trimmed her again. The crowd, half of them soaked by this shower, clapped and cheered nevertheless, while some broke into song, and cars parked all around the airfield flashed their lights in farewell. The roar of the engines increased to a bellow. The figures up there on the promenade deck waved. Slowly the airship moved clear of the tower and began to gain height, and, making a last slow circuit of the Royal Airship Works, the R 101 flew heavily away to the south. Rain began to fall, and a gusty wind blew across the fields as the crowds dispersed from Cardington.

• • •

All over southeast England people turned out, despite the weather, to see the airship on its way to France. Many of them were disappointed, even disturbed, by the spectacle, for the airship seemed to be flying very sluggishly—her engines sounded, so one eyewitness thought, "weak and unbusinesslike," and her speed seemed no more than twenty-five miles an hour. Soon after nine, though, a reassuring radio message was received at Cardington. The R 101 was crossing the coast near Hastings, flying at 54.2 knots and gradually gaining height. "Ship behaving well generally," it said.

Certainly to the passengers all seemed satisfactory. They were on their way as scheduled. The dinner may not have been up to Cunard standards, but it was adequate. The ship seemed to roll somewhat, but then it was a rough and windy night. After dinner some of them sat in the huge lounge, while others went to the smoking room; but most of them were tired, there was nothing to see through the rain-smeared windows, and before long all were in bed. "After an excellent supper," said a second message, "our distinguished passengers smoked a final cigar, and having sighted the

French coast, have gone to bed after the excitement of their leave-taking. The crew have settled down to watch-keeping routine."

But the watchkeeping that night was not all routine. The weather forecast was ominous—winds of forty to fifty miles an hour, twice as strong as they had expected—and almost from the start the R 101 was rolling and pitching seriously. Within an hour of departure there was a fault in the aft engine, and for three hours they had to struggle against the rising storm with only four. The ship never rose more than a thousand feet, so that they very nearly hit a house on high ground in Hertfordshire and could see the dim white of the waves below all the way across the Channel. Over France the weather grew worse. The drizzle developed into gusty squalls, and the winds strengthened as forecast. Sometimes the R 101 was blown almost sideways by their force; sometimes it may even have been moving backward.

In these conditions Irwin had no intention of crossing the Alps, as Lord Thomson had envisaged. He plotted a route that would take them over Paris to Toulouse, reaching the Mediterranean some time the following morning. From time to time the crew inspected the gasbags, clambering along the ropewalks that crisscrossed the interior of the envelope. So strong was the wind by now

SISTER SHIP

UNDERWOOD AND UNDERWOOD

Bitter rivalry existed between the builders of the R 101 and the designers of the second airship of the fleet, the R 100 (above, at Cardington). Though the R 100 was a successful design (she made a round trip to Canada), the imperial fleet was never completed.

that everything in there creaked, groaned, and hissed as they worked, the gasbags squelched themselves into new shapes as the pressure shifted inside them, and the metal harnesses that supported them clanked and chafed in the darkness. The night outside was very black now; only occasionally did a dim light show from the ground below through the drifting cloud and the mist.

Shortly after two in the morning the radio operator exchanged messages with the airport at Le Bourget and confirmed that the R 101 was near Beauvais, a market city some eighty miles north of the capital. She was flying very slowly, shaken all over by the wind. Soon afterward an engineer in one of the nacelles looked through his window into the darkness and saw an astonishing thing. Protruding grotesquely out of the rainy mist, only a few yards away from the airship, was the humped roof of a building, a massive grayish object stuck about with pinnacles, very old, very stark. For a few seconds he saw it there, as the airship labored by, and then it was lost again in the rain and the dark. It was the roof of Beauvais Cathedral.

The engineer scarcely had time to tell his companion when the airship gave an abrupt lurch, dropped, recovered, dropped again, and with a terrific shudder was suddenly still. There was a moment's pause: then suddenly a tremendous breaking roar, a frenzied ringing of bells, a clatter of feet, and the shout of an officer somewhere—"We're down, lads! We're down!"

• • •

A few people in Beauvais had seen the airship pass. Everyone had read about it, but few got out of bed when, in the small hours, they heard the rumble of the engines through the noise of the storm. Those who did saw only a dim line of lights passing slowly through the rain—slightly crablike, some people thought, as though the wind were skewing the aircraft around. Some saw all the lights go off and on again, and one witness reported sparks flying from one of the engines.

One man alone saw the end of the

R101. M. Alfred Rabouille was a factory worker, but as a sideline he used to snare rabbits in the woods on the outskirts of Beauvais, and that night he braved the weather to set his traps in the Bois des Coutumes, a line of hazel woods along a ridge some three miles out of the city. This is rolling, limestone country, still to this day remarkably rural and unfrequented, though the city silhouette is visible from the ridge, and the busy Paris road is only a mile or two away. Some of the ground is plowed, some is rough pasture, almost downland, and it is accessible only by rough tracks, and bleak when the wind is raw. That night it must have been particularly unwelcoming, as the rain streamed down and the wind blew in savage gusts, and Rabouille was understandably frightened when he saw the dim shape of the airship laboring toward him.

For it was very low, perhaps 150 feet up, and it was flying very slowly, its engines thudding heavily, directly toward the wood. The Frenchman watched aghast. The wind was blowing the airship sideways, closer still to him; but when it was some 300 yards away a gust seemed to make it lurch and dip, its nose failed to clear the ridge, and with hideous crashing and rending noises it plunged into the trees along the hillside. Almost at once there was a deafening explosion, knocking Rabouille to the ground, and then a vast column of fire rose into the sky. Rabouille could see figures moving "like madmen" to and fro in the flames, but he was too terrified to go closer, and, running wildly away into the woods, he stumbled back through the darkness, pursued always by the flicker of the flames, to his own cottage down the hill.

All but eight men on the R101 died in the accident; two more died later of their burns. Lord Thomson, Sir Sefton Brancker, Irwin, the representatives of the Indian and Australian governments, the designers and chief constructors of the great airship—all died and are forgotten. So catastrophic was the tragedy, so humiliating to British pride, that the Imperial Airship Scheme was aban-

doned: the R100 was broken up, the apparatus of the route was dismantled, and the empire never did see the grand spectacle of the dirigibles dipping their ensigns over Bermuda or Singapore. No more British airships were built: the field was left to the Germans once more, with their *Graf Spee* and *Hindenburg*, until tragedy overcame them too, and the whole breed of intercontinental airships passed into legend and conjecture.

Just why the R101 failed was never satisfactorily determined. Some experts thought it broke up in the air because of structural weakness—caused by the extra midships section, perhaps. Others thought it failed through lack of power. Still others maintained that no one error of design, but a whole series of them, contributed to the disaster. Mysteries of many kinds came to surround the story. A medium claimed to have authentic messages from Irwin, attributing the crash to insufficient lifting power—messages so convincingly detailed that many skeptics came to accept them as genuine. It was said that at two that night Irwin's telephone receiver on his desk at Cardington inexplicably rang through to the station exchange; that at the same moment there was an unexplained knock at the door of the first officer's house; that both Ramsay MacDonald and Sefton Brancker had presentiments of disaster.

As for the airship itself, nothing was left but a colossal pile of metalwork on the edge of the wood at Beauvais; the only piece of fabric to survive was the

Fifty-four men were aboard the R101 when it crashed and burned near Beauvais on October 5, 1930, and six, including the bandaged crewman above, survived. A few hours after the accident, the skeletal wreckage opposite was all that remained of an imperial dream.

tattered RAF ensign that flew high in the stern. Two of the preposterous pillars from the lounge were left standing grotesquely among the carnage. The skeleton was broken up eventually and taken back to England, where it was used to make kitchenware in Sheffield. The charred bodies of the airship's crew and passengers were taken home to England by a destroyer of the Royal Navy, and after a funeral procession through London were buried amid national mourning at Cardington. There to this day, within sight of the airship sheds, their common tomb is carefully tended, and inside the church there hang the remnants of the airship's flag, brought home from Beauvais with its dead.

An impressive monument was erected on the Beauvais-to-Paris road, where the passing English motorist, on his way from Calais to the capital, may still glimpse its sad roster: Brigadier General the Right Honorable Lord Thomson of Cardington, P.C., C.B.E., D.S.O.; Air Vice Marshal Sir W. S. Brancker, K.C.B., A.F.C.; the four squadron leaders; the lieutenant colonel; the wing commander; the two majors; the lieutenant commander; and all the coxswains, riggers, engineers, wireless operators, and stewards who made the fateful flight that October evening long ago, down to J. W. Megginson, galley boy, and James Buck, valet.

On the actual site of the crash, though, a mile or two away over the fields and woods, there is a less grandiose memorial. It is a small and timeworn concrete pillar, half hidden on the edge of the Bois des Coutumes. From a distance it does not show at all, and even when you reach it, scrambling through the scratchy undergrowth and pushing aside the hazel branches, there is nothing much to see—only that stumpy gray obelisk and the brief inscription:

LE DIRIGEABLE
R101
5 OCTOBRE 1930

Jan Morris, a regular contributor to these pages and a world traveler, has not been around it in a dirigible—but who knows?

Victor Hugo's Wayward Daughter

Adèle's secret diary,
the basis for Truffaut's haunting film,
sheds some light
on her obsessive and unrequited passion

François Truffaut's film *The Story of Adèle H.* is a classic account of a woman obsessed. It is about Victor Hugo's daughter, who developed such a stubborn passion for a young English officer that she left her family and followed him to distant garrisons in Nova Scotia and Barbados. She had a mission to accomplish, and nothing —not her family's pleas for her return, not the young Englishman's clear indifference, not her own deteriorating mental state—would stop her.

Truffaut recently told me that he is drawn to characters like Adèle for whom love is an irreversible and lifelong commitment. In his films this "definitive love," as he calls it, is sometimes hard on the partner, for example, the husband in *The Soft Skin*, who is fatally shot by his wife as he is lunching with his mistress. Adèle is another of these Truffaut women who play for keeps. As she says in the film: "One doesn't change one's father or one's mother, and one doesn't change one's husband." Truffaut also wanted to make a film based on history, a reconstituted documentary in which nothing would be invented. Adèle Hugo existed. The incidents in the film and the dia-

Isabelle Adjani, above with François Truffaut, stars in The Story of Adèle H. *The real Adèle Hugo, opposite, was about twenty-five when this photograph was taken at the Hugo home in Guernsey.*

logue are based on documented material, for Adèle Hugo kept a diary that was exhaustive in its detail. In 1969 when Truffaut came across the first published volume of it, he knew he had to make his film.

Adèle Hugo's diary begins in 1852, when her father was in exile on Jersey, one of the Channel Islands. She became Victor Hugo's Boswell, taking down his conversation verbatim. She also wrote entries of a more personal nature—often in a code that consisted of scrambling the syllables of words, so that "table," for instance, became "bleta." The diary ends in 1862, when Adèle left

the second of the Hugo residences-in-exile at Guernsey.

Adèle's writings reveal her as a woman driven to madness by inner conflicts: she worshiped her father but felt a need to exist in her own right; she had feminist leanings (she wrote to her English lieutenant, Albert Pinson, that she found marriage "a humiliating thing for a woman" and that she would never give up the good fortune of being called Miss Hugo, just as Miss Molière, Miss Shakespeare, Miss Byron, and Miss Dante would never have changed their famous names), but her feminist platform was soon jettisoned, and she devoted ten years of her life to a vain effort to become Mrs. Pinson. Adèle felt also that she was in some curious way ahead of her time. She called herself "a woman of the nineteenth century addressing herself to the twentieth century." She would write a book "that will not be laughed at in a hundred years."

Her diary is that book. In it she wrote a moving statement of intent:

That incredible thing, that a young woman so cloistered that she cannot go out alone five minutes to buy a newspaper, will walk on the sea, will move over the sea, will pass from the old world to the new to join her lover—that thing I will accomplish.

That incredible thing, that a young woman who has no other means than her father's charity, will have, four years from now, gold in both pockets, honest gold, her gold—that thing I will accomplish.

That incredible thing, that a woman living under the same roof with a man she loves passionately [she does not mean her father, as we shall see], leaves him, without scenes and despair—that thing I will accomplish.

Here is Adèle Hugo's story, as much of it as we know from the Hugo family records, Victor Hugo's biographers, and the three volumes of her journals that have thus far been edited.

Adèle Hugo was born on July 28, 1830, the youngest of Victor Hugo's five children. The oldest, Léopold, had died at the age of two months. Next came Léopoldine, then Charles, then François Victor. Adèle was a pretty child, with large, round brown eyes. She liked to read and she played the piano. But her father's favorite daughter was the more vivacious Léopoldine.

In February, 1843, when she was nineteen, Léopoldine married Charles Vacquerie, a young businessman from a shipping family in Le Havre. In September they took a racing dinghy out on the Seine in windy weather and were both drowned. Adèle was thirteen at the time, and her adolescence became enveloped by the memory of her dead sister. Léopoldine's photographs were placed in every room of the house. The dress she had drowned in was on exhibit. Her father always kept one of Léopoldine's handkerchiefs in his pocket. Now that she was her father's only daughter, Adèle must have felt that she had to replace Léopoldine. In Truffaut's film Adèle tells a small boy she meets in the Halifax bank that her name is Léopoldine, and she also has a recurring nightmare about Léopoldine drowning.

On December 2, 1851, Louis Napoleon, the prince-president of France's short-lived Second Republic, staged a coup d'état.

Victor Hugo, who had been politically active for several years, tried to organize the resistance to the coup and was expelled from the country on December 11 with seventy-one other *proscrits* (proscribed ones). At the time, his two sons were in the Conciergerie prison, for together with Auguste Vacquerie, the brother of Charles Vacquerie, they had founded *L'Evénement*, a newspaper that was opposed to Louis Napoleon.

In 1851, when Victor Hugo left France for what would be nineteen years of exile, he was one of the most famous men in Europe. In a day that lacked movie stars or television stars or rock stars, poets were stars; as the poet-politician banished for his courageous stand, Hugo was a superstar. His every move was front-page news in France. His works sold out almost as soon as they were put on sale. A prominent Parisian hostess wrote him: "I would like to wash your feet, spread perfume over them, and wipe them with my hair." When his furniture was sold after his banishment, delirious fans mobbed his house. No wonder the term "Hugolatry" was coined. As the superstar's daughter, Adèle was proud of her father's fame but yearned for evidence of her own personal worth. She is a predecessor of the troubled children of the famous in our own time, such as Diana Barrymore or Patty Hearst.

Hugo left France for Brussels and was soon joined by his mistress Juliette Drouet. He wrote to his wife in Paris: "Tell my little Adèle that I don't want her to grow pale and thin. She must be calm. The future is all to the good." On July 25, 1852, he wrote Adèle directly:

Do you know that I am going to see you again? I am going to cross the ocean, and so are you, and we will meet in a place that is calm, free, and charming. There we will wait for the end of the bad play that is on at the moment, and we will bless God, who, having taken away our country, leaves us our family.

Hugo's children were all adults (Adèle was twenty-two, and her brothers were older) and could have been leading their own lives, but Hugo in exile required the emotional comfort of a full family setting. He left for the British-ruled island of Jersey in July, 1852, and was joined by Adèle and her mother. They found a three-story house on the sea called Marine Terrace. They were also joined by the two sons, who had been released from prison, and by Auguste Vacquerie. Hugo, whose energy was superhuman, could not stand inactivity. Everyone had to keep busy, and Marine Terrace soon became a literary factory, with Charles working on novels, François Victor translating the complete works of Shakespeare, Mme Hugo writing a book about her husband, Auguste Vacquerie doing political articles, while Adèle took down what everybody said in her diary, which she had just begun.

At the age of sixteen, identifying with the dead Léopoldine, Adèle had taken Auguste Vacquerie as her lover. On March 28, 1852, she wrote:

Alas, sometimes I regret my past, my candor, the beauty of my soul, my first love, my first impressions, the organ, the Place Royale, Villequier [the Vacquerie home], its fine garden lit by moonlight in 1846 (six years already), Auguste and the dizziness of our first kisses, when loving and grandiose, I sacrificed my [illegible: serenity, virginity?] to his happiness.

When Auguste Vacquerie went into exile with the Hugos, he continued his affair with Adèle. The entry in her diary for October 6, 1854, records the following exchange:

Léopoldine, eldest daughter of Victor Hugo, and her young husband, Charles Vacquerie, drowned in a boating accident on the Seine in 1843—an event that would particularly darken Adèle's own life.

36

Auguste: "I do not want your body without your heart. I will not treat you like a streetwalker. I intend to respect you more."

Adèle: "I gave myself to you because you were suffering. Prostitution can be a form of sublime devotion. How can we know that the streetwalker is not really a sister of charity?"

Later, when she fell in love with Albert Pinson, Adèle found Auguste's presence an embarrassment and asked her mother to persuade him to go back to France. However, he remained in the Hugo entourage, and when Adèle wrote of living under the same roof with a man she loves passionately, and then leaving him, she was referring to Auguste.

The household at Jersey was geared entirely to Victor Hugo's routine. The great man rose at dawn, ate two raw eggs for breakfast, and worked all morning. After lunch he would get up, saying: *"Post prandium passus mille"* (after meals, a thousand steps), and walk to the post office to mail his letters. Then more work, or visits from other members of the exile colony. Adèle, with few friends her own age, was surrounded by elderly men talking politics. Exile was gloomy and the whole family felt it. On August 23, 1854, Adèle recorded something her brother Charles had said: "I won't miss Jersey. I will not be any sorrier to leave it than I was to leave the Conciergerie."

Adèle kept busy, transcribing conversations, playing the piano several hours a day, and writing music. She exchanged French lessons for English lessons with the son of the Hugos' landlord, Mr. Rose, whom she identifies only as J. It was probably at the Roses' house that Adèle heard for the first time about Albert Pinson, a young officer visiting Jersey who had seen her and wanted to meet her. No one knows when Adèle finally did meet Pinson, but meet him she did, for in the summer of 1854 he is mentioned in the diary six times as a visitor to Marine Terrace.

Then an ensign in the West Yorkshire militia, he was blond, with a pretty, girlish face, long sideburns, and a reputa-

Hugo dominated his family as he did literary France. Above, he strikes a pose with Adèle's lover, Auguste Vacquerie (bearded). At right, he sits with his wife (center), Adèle (left), and his sons, François Victor (front) and Charles.

tion as a dandy, a snob, and an inveterate gambler. He told Adèle that he had been offered the choice between the militia and debtor's prison.

On August 21, 1854, Pinson was invited to Marine Terrace for lunch with the entire Hugo family. They discussed politics, as usual, and in Adèle's transcription of the conversation Pinson hardly got a word in. One can imagine him, overpolite, content to be a good listener, intimidated before the imposing figure of Victor Hugo. Hugo for his part was not impressed with his daughter's suitor, but still he wanted her to marry. "That is a woman's role," he told her.

When Adèle and Albert discussed marriage, Pinson pleaded lack of money. "That's not a reason," Adèle wrote to him. "After my marriage, I will have a fortune: 40,000 francs, 2,000 a year. My family has no right to tell me how to spend my money." Pinson argued that he would be called a coward if he left the army. "You will resign your commission," Adèle wrote, "we will get married, and with my dowry you will buy a more important, more lucrative, more brilliant commission as a line officer. No one can accuse a man who leaves the nondangerous militia for a commission in the line of being a coward."

Having known him six months, Adèle had decided that she wanted Albert Pinson for a husband, and no other. She began to devise complicated stratagems

to bring him around to her views. In a letter addressed to Pinson in England in December, 1854, she explained why she had first attempted suicide and then pretended to be pregnant by him:

At that time . . . I had to tear you away from the army, at any price. I had to save, at any price, your moral and physical being.

It was clear that after having reasoned with you in vain, I had to use other means. I had two possibilities—my death, and your jealousy. I tried the first, without success. Afraid that time was running out, and that some military decision would send you away, I tried the second. . . . The letter was sent. It said that I had had a child by you, but had not dared tell you because of your cowardly conduct toward me, and that I was marrying a handsome and witty young man. The only way to stop the marriage was to give up your commission. I realized, from something you had written in your second letter, that *you intended to ask me to accept your hand*, without giving up your commission. . . . Also, at that time, it was absolutely impossible for me to marry, first because I had to be an example for my sex in the struggle against prejudice; second because I would have broken the heart of Mr. Auguste and my poor mother; and third, because I would do anything rather than give my hand to a man [illegible] years younger than myself, who preferred "something, even if that something is honor," to me; and finally, because before choosing a man, even for a lover, and before giving him any rights over me, I would have to make him prove the depth and value of his love.

We can only imagine Pinson's reaction. In any case, after 1856, when he was transferred to the Sixteenth Foot Regiment in Bedfordshire, he did not see much of her. In 1858 he was promoted to lieutenant and sent to Ireland, where he remained until 1861. Adèle went through periods of depression and apathy, which made her father impatient. She was over twenty-five, an age when proper young women were meant to be married. He said she was self-centered, but Mme Hugo defended her. "That Adèle is temperamentally cold, may seem to suffer from a sort of dryness," she told her husband, "is perfectly possible; but have we any right to expect that a girl to whom the joys of love have been refused, in whose nature there is no harmony, who is incomplete, should be like others of her sex? Who knows what she has suffered, may still be suffering. . . ." Exile, Mme Hugo went on, was bad for Adèle.

In 1856 Adèle had a nervous breakdown that may have been connected to Pinson's transfer. The doctor told her to stop playing the piano. In 1859 Mme Hugo took Adèle to Paris, where she could have a more amusing social life. They stayed four months and then they traveled to England. Perhaps she saw Pinson again, for he was then stationed in Ireland. That same year, Napoleon III offered amnesty to all political exiles; Hugo, who had moved with his family from Jersey to the island of Guernsey, did not take advantage of the offer. "When freedom returns to France," he wrote, "I will return."

Adèle was increasingly cranky and sullen. She had suitors but turned them down. Her mother continued to take her on trips to France and Belgium. In December, 1861, she told her parents that she was engaged to Pinson, and he came to Hauteville House, the Hugos' new home at Guernsey, during the Christmas holidays. After they parted, she fell again into a state of depression. In January, 1862, Pinson's regiment was transferred to Halifax, Nova Scotia.

Adèle Hugo began keeping her diary in 1852 while living with her family at Marine Terrace, above, in Jersey. Here she was courted by Lt. Albert Pinson, who proved to be her undoing.

Meanwhile Hugo's family was deserting him. Mme Hugo sometimes spent nine months of the year on the Continent. Charles had married and was living in Paris, and François Victor had moved to Brussels.

On June 2, 1863, Victor Hugo wrote the following entry in his diary: "M. Th. de C. [Tommaso Cannizzaro, an Italian poet] asked Adèle's hand in marriage. She refused. Marriages successively refused by her: Mezaize—Busquet—Prince Pignatelli—Th. de Canizzario [sic]—Bancel."

On June 18 Adèle left Guernsey for England. She wrote her father that she was joining her fiancé in Malta but promised not to marry without her parents' consent. On June 30 her father learned through a friend in England that she had left not for Malta but for Halifax. "She hates me," he cried to his son François Victor.

Arriving in Halifax aboard the 25,000-ton steamship Great Eastern—this is the opening scene of Truffaut's film—Adèle stayed first at the Hotel Halifax, where she was known as "the French miss." She gave her name as Miss Lewly. She soon found lodgings with a warm, friendly couple named Saunders. Mr. Saunders was a messenger for the Union Bank and worked nights as a waiter at banquets. Complaining about the high cost of living in Halifax, Adèle asked her father to send her 400 francs a month. He sent her only 150 francs a month, with a semiannual clothing allowance of 300 francs, and grumbled that he had now become "Adèle's banker."

On September 17 Adèle wrote her mother that she was now Mrs. Pinson:

I am married and am still under the excitement of the event. . . . my name can be spelled with an *e* or with an *i*. . . . I do not and will not live in the barracks or camps that these gentlemen are in. . . . I have and will have my lodgings in town like the other ladies, and our husbands will visit us. . . . Please try to attenuate the sadness that Mr. ——— will feel when he hears about my marriage.

The Hugos chose to believe that their wandering daughter had finally settled into a wifely role, and Victor Hugo placed a wedding announcement in the Guernsey *Gazette* of October 9, 1863, adding the fictional detail that Pinson had distinguished himself in the Crimean War. On October 10, 1863, Hugo wrote his publisher, Pierre Jules Hetzel:

My daughter has become an Englishwoman. Such are the blows of exile! Her husband is a veteran of the Crimea, a young English officer, aristocratic, a stickler for propriety, gentilhomme and a gentleman. . . . the young people are now on their way to Halifax. Between my son-in-law and myself there lies the temperamental distance that separates the French and the English, and the physical distance that lies between Europe and America. But there is such a thing as a right to happiness. My daughter has claimed it, and I cannot blame her.

Adèle had reasoned that the marriage, once announced, would have to take place: another maneuver to capture Pinson. But finally in November, 1863, she admitted in a letter to her brother François Victor that she was not married. When Hugo got the news, he blamed Pinson rather than Adèle. Convinced that his daughter had been jilted, he wrote his wife on December 1:

The man is a ruffian, the lowest of the low! . . . Adèle deserves our congratulations—for it is the greatest good luck imaginable that she has not married. . . . My only wish now is that she may be quickly returned to us. We will say that since the marriage was not registered before the French consul, it is null and void in France. . . . In six months' time Adèle will be back at Hauteville. The only difference will be that she will go by the name of

Mme Adèle. She is of a suitable age to be "belady'd," and we are answerable to no one. She has only to get quit of that scamp and return to us. Thereafter, I will take charge. She will forget, and she will get well. The poor child has never yet been happy; it is high time that she started. I will give some parties for her at Hauteville House, to which I will invite the most intelligent persons I can lay my hands on. I will dedicate books to Adèle. I will make of her the crown of my old age. I will glorify her exile. . . . Later, when she is cured and cheerful, we will find a decent, honorable husband for her. Let us dismiss the memory of this type of the licentious soldiery.

Surely Hugo meant well, but there is something richly comic in the notion that because they came from him, book dedications would be an effective form of therapy for Adèle.

Pinson soon wrote François Victor to explain his side of things. He insisted that "I have never fallen short of the standards of honor, have never encouraged any hopes in Mlle Hugo, have never asked for her hand in marriage." Pinson asked François Victor to have her brought home as quickly as possible.

François Victor realized that this would be no easy task. In one letter Adèle had confided that she planned to kidnap Pinson and in another that she had found a magician to hypnotize him. François Victor wrote his mother:

She [Adèle] is more obstinate than ever about marrying the man against his will. She has even found a magnetizer who would accomplish the operation. . . . the operation would cost 5,000 francs, which she prays my father to advance on her dowry. The magnetizer would only be paid if he succeeded. Besides the magnetizer, she would need, all ready for the ceremony, two witnesses and a minister. As you can see, the poor child is losing her mind in the pursuit of her pathetic ideal.

The Saunderses were concerned about their mysterious lodger. She ate almost nothing and went out in the sub-zero Halifax winter without a coat. The officer she was planning to marry had come to see her only two or three times. She went regularly to the Bank of British North America on Hollis Street to collect bank drafts, but she lived like a pauper (she must have given money to Pinson, still a sportsman and a gambler, and still debt-ridden).

Then one day, quite by accident, Mrs. Saunders learned who the mysterious young woman really was. The French cook in the household of General Sir Charles Hastings Doyle, British commander in chief in Halifax, dropped by to hire Mr. Saunders for a gala dinner. Noticing a letter ready to be mailed, he asked in astonishment, "Who in this house writes letters to Victor Hugo?" Mrs. Saunders said it was her lodger, Miss Lewly. "But do you know who Victor Hugo is?" the cook asked. "He is the greatest writer in France."

The letter was actually addressed to François Victor, and Mrs. Saunders began writing to him. François Victor replied and sent warm clothing for his sister. In one of his few surviving letters, published in the Halifax *Morning Herald* on June 2, 1885 (the year of Victor Hugo's death), François Victor wrote: "Tell me also in your letter how I can repay you for the stamps you use. I can indeed very easily repay you for those trifling expenses, but never for your Christian kindness."

No member of the close-knit Hugo family went to retrieve Adèle. Aboard the *Great Eastern*, the trip from Southampton to Halifax was not very difficult or very long. Adèle's mother wanted to go but was in poor health, and everyone else was too busy. There seemed to be a curious apathy at work: the Hugo family got used to the situation and while lamenting it, did nothing about it. They may have feared the decision facing them if their irrational daughter did return.

Adèle left the Saunderses in the winter of 1864 and eventually moved to a small farm two miles from Halifax. She rarely went out or saw anyone. Stories about her that have been handed down say that she would show up, uninvited, in her finest gown when there was a ball at Bellevue, General Doyle's residence. She would ask to see Pinson, who would take her aside, talk to her a few minutes, and then leave her. Sometimes she dressed like a man and hid behind the trees of Grafton Park, across from Bellevue, to watch Pinson and whatever young woman he was escorting.

At some point, probably in 1865, Pinson became engaged to Agnes Johnstone, the daughter of Judge James W. Johnstone, chief of the Tory party and former prime minister of Nova Scotia. It would have been a brilliant match for the young officer. But Adèle went to see her lawyer, Robert Motton, and told him that she and Pinson had been secretly married in England before Albert had come to Halifax. She was Pinson's true wife and would never allow him to marry anyone else. Motton informed Judge Johnstone that he had a client who claimed to be Pinson's wife. In Victorian Halifax this was enough to break the engagement. (In the film Truffaut changes the story a bit; Adèle goes

A volume of Adèle's diary

The publication of Adèle Hugo's diary, which led to the François Truffaut film *The Story of Adèle H.*, was the result of another, but less destructive, obsession. In 1955 Frances Vernor Guille, a professor at Wooster College in Ohio, heard about the diary from descendants of the Hugo family when she was researching her doctorate on Victor Hugo's son François Victor. She found parts of the diary among the papers at the Maison de Victor Hugo in Paris and another part in the Pierpont Morgan Library in New York. Miss Guille began the difficult task of deciphering and dating the diaries and published the first volume, which covers the year 1852, in Paris in 1968 and the second volume, of 1853, in 1971. She had finished piecing together the third volume, of 1854, when she died in January, 1976, at the age of sixty-eight, leaving her labors unfinished. The last eight years of the diaries still remain to be edited. Miss Guille had served as a consultant to Truffaut and gave him the typescript of the third volume, which Truffaut graciously lent to me. —T.M.

directly to the judge's house and tells him she is pregnant with Pinson's child.)

In June, 1866, Pinson's regiment was transferred to Barbados, the English army headquarters for the West Indies. Adèle followed. One of the few clues to her life there comes from an anonymous letter to the editor published on May 27, 1885, in the New York *Tribune* in connection with Victor Hugo's death:

I am writing from memories of boyhood and I am therefore unable to fix the exact dates; but I think it was somewhere about 1860 to 1863 that there came to the island a stranger, a woman of the most striking appearance. She was tall and beautiful, with black hair and a pair of black eyes that used to frighten me. . . . her dress added to her remarkableness; it was not the light dress of the tropics, but heavy velvets, silks, and even furs at some times, clothed her. All this spoke of a home far away to the North; a home lost and a mind given up to some strange fantasy. Her once brilliant costumes were faded and uncared for; and her tall figure was robbed of half its grace by habiliments so unsuited.

She took a room with a Mrs. Chadderton, the letter said. She was always writing and had boxes of manuscripts. She became known as Mrs. Pinson. "Everyone realized that in her heart was written some untold history of sorrow." Her name was linked with a "Captain" or a "Colonel" Pinson. (In 1867 Pinson had been promoted to captain.) Adjacent to the Barbados barracks was a race track where the local Derby was run. Several English officers competed in the Derby, and among them was Pinson. "He had a horse to do wonders," the letter went on, "though I don't think the horse actually did much. His master was a more wonderful creature, according to current gossip, and a little 'jockeying' was accredited to him. After some time, this sad, wild-eyed woman was lost sight of."

Pinson had seduced Adèle. He had accepted money from her. He may have even promised her marriage. But in the end one comes to pity Pinson as he is hounded from garrison to garrison. Truffaut told Bruce Robinson, the actor

Adèle Hugo lies on her deathbed in 1915. Her bizarre journey in pursuit of Pinson had ended in 1872, and she spent the rest of her life in a rest home outside of Paris.

who portrayed Pinson in *The Story of Adèle H.*, to play the English lieutenant as a victim more than a villain. "Just remember," Truffaut said, "that no man can stand being loved one hundred per cent. And remember that every morning when the lieutenant wakes up, he is terrified that he is going to find Adèle dead on his doorstep."

In 1869 Pinson's regiment left Barbados for Dublin. This time Adèle did not follow. She seems by then to have suffered a complete mental collapse. She never saw Pinson again. In 1870 he sold his commission and married a lieutenant colonel's daughter.

In the same year that Pinson married, France went to war with Prussia and capitulated several months later. Napoleon III was deposed, and Victor Hugo, upon his return from exile, was elected deputy in the new National Assembly. From his homeland he continued to communicate with Adèle through François Victor, to whom he wrote on March 27, 1870: "Have you told Adèle that my arms are open?"

In Barbados Adèle was finally identified as Victor Hugo's daughter by a black woman, Celine Alvarez Baa, who brought her back to France and her family at her own expense. Adèle and Mme Baa arrived in Paris in February, 1872. Adèle was forty-two years old. Her father was seventy, still so sexually active in his old age that his mistress had him watched by a private detective. In his diary for February 23, he wrote of a meeting with Mme Baa, whom he described as *"la primera negra de mi vida"* (the first Negress of my life). Hugo gave Mme Baa 1,500 francs, as well as some of Adèle's jewelry.

Adèle must have been in a sorry state, for her father immediately sent her to a rest home in the Paris suburb of Saint-Mandé. The entry for March 16 in Hugo's diary says:

I went to Saint-Mandé, Grande Rue 106, with Dr. E. Allix. She [Adèle] is very calm and very sweet; she kissed my hands and said: I am content. She is still convinced that invisible persons talk to her. . . . she refused to wear her new slippers. I told her: "My daughter, put them on." She obeyed. I had a piano brought to her. She plays a little and writes a great deal, but did not want to show me what she wrote. The doctors suggest I space out my visits.

In 1876 Adèle asked her father to obtain her release, but he refused. She remained confined for the rest of her long life, another forty-three years. In the meantime Hugo's two sons had died, and the old lion himself gave up the ghost in 1885. He died a wealthy man and left half his fortune, four million francs, to Adèle. As a result of her inheritance, she was transferred to the Château de Suresnes, a luxurious nursing home, where she occupied an entire pavilion. She remained a tireless pianist and claimed the great operas as her compositions. Her death in 1915 went almost unnoticed.

Was Adèle destined for madness? Had Pinson not existed, would she have found some other target? There was in Adèle's character an exaggerated fixity of purpose that set her apart from what we think of as "normal." Her compulsions took the shape of a tidy equation: Mlle Hugo would become Mme Pinson. Her effort to achieve the impossible, her self-deception, finally caused her to break down. Perhaps the most moving scene in Truffaut's film is near the end, when Adèle, distraught and mumbling, weaves down an alley in Barbados, crosses Pinson's path, and fails to recognize him as he calls out her name. By that time her obsession no longer depended on him. It had become self-sustaining. □

Ted Morgan wrote about Stavisky—the man and the film—in the Summer issue.

In Truffaut's film a crazed and defeated Adèle passes Lieutenant Pinson (Bruce Robinson) on a street in Barbados without recognizing him.

Outwitting
the Final Solution

One of the miracles of
World War II is that several hundred Jews
survived—at large—in Berlin.
Some of them, who live there still,
recollect those years

The synagogue on Fasanenstrasse, above, was set afire on Kristallnacht,
November 9, 1938, when full-scale destruction of Jewish property began.

By RUTH GAY

"It was our duty not to permit ourselves to be slaughtered like cattle by the Nazis."

In May, 1975, Germans celebrated the thirtieth anniversary of the end of World War II, which also brought the end of their domination by Hitler. I was living in Berlin at the time, and I could hardly go anywhere without hearing the conversation turn to those last days of the war. People recalled many long-buried events, among them the startling fact that some fourteen hundred Jews had survived the war years in Berlin. In a city where hardly one stone stood on another by the spring of 1945, their survival—in spite of Hitler's determination to eradicate them—seemed to me nearly miraculous.

Today much of the community life of Berlin's five thousand Jews takes place in a modest building on Fasanenstrasse, on the site of the synagogue destroyed by the Nazis in November, 1938. At a meeting of the women's club there I met Frau Neubauer, an energetic and attractive woman of seventy-seven, who, it turned out, was one of the fourteen hundred who had survived. I asked her whether she knew any others. She glanced around the room and pointed out three other women who, like her, came on Tuesday afternoons to drink coffee and chat with friends. In the short time I was in Berlin I met a dozen Jews who had remained in the city during the war. They were as various as any dozen people chosen at random in a large city could be. Few of them had been involved in politics before the war, and none of them had chosen to be heroes.

When the Nazis came to power in January, 1933, Berlin's population of more than four million included 160,000 Jews. By the outbreak of the war nearly seven years later, emigration had reduced the Jewish community to 82,000. All of them knew they faced a desperate future. As the Nazi plan for a "final solution" began to crystallize, they fell, eventually, into three groups. A major-

ity, officially registered as members of the Jewish community, were gradually deported according to the Nazis' carefully arranged timetable. A small number, either married to Christians and childless, or raising their children as Christians, were exempted for a time from persecution. Finally, about five thousand Berlin Jews, in an effort to disappear within the city, went underground. From these came the fourteen hundred who managed to survive.

The first widespread arrests of Jews occurred in November, 1938, during a nationwide pogrom that came to be known as the Kristallnacht (night of glass) because of the broken plate glass that soon littered the streets of German towns and cities. Jewish business premises were smashed, synagogues were destroyed, nearly one hundred Jews were killed, and about thirty thousand Jewish men were arrested. The brutality and scale of the violence dramatically forecast the persecution that followed. Already harsh decrees were intensified, increasing the physical hardships of the Jews' daily existence and isolating them from their Gentile neighbors. Gentiles who helped Jewish friends were, at the very least, called names, the favorite Nazi epithet being *Judenknecht* (lackey of the Jews). Soon any contact between Jew and Gentile became dangerous: a storekeeper selling a forbidden item to a Jew was fined or imprisoned; a public official lenient with a Jew could be deprived of his pension. By the late stages of the war, when things were going badly for Hitler's Reich, *Judenknechte* were even shot. Despite these dangers, many Gentiles remained friendly with Jews; indeed, for every Jew who survived in Berlin, there was a handful of Gentiles who, either by their silence or by their active help, made existence possible.

Freedom was of course the *sine qua*

non of survival. Those who were captured and sent off in the boxcars had little chance, no matter how clever, resourceful, and brave they were. But eluding capture required a tough constitution. As the historian of the Berlin Jewish community, H. G. Sellenthin, has recorded: "Many had no real home and spent their nights in waiting rooms or toilets. Some slept at friends' houses during the day." It was dangerous to hide people at night, since searchers from the Gestapo nearly always arrived in the small hours of the morning.

Then there was the sheer boredom of remaining hidden. "Even those who had a place to stay," writes Sellenthin, "could not stand the confinement. They would go out and then get picked up by a patrol. Men particularly were in danger because the patrols were looking for deserters." Members of the patrols, which might appear suddenly anywhere in Berlin, wore heavy chains around their necks as part of their uniform. The sardonic Berliners promptly dubbed them *Kettenhunde* (chain dogs).

The Nazi machine pursued its course with a hypnotizing "pedantry of murder," in the words of the German writer and politician Theodor Heuss. Its victims were caught up in an endless round of detail. Although the Jews who remained in Berlin eventually came to realize that they lived under an ultimate sentence of death, they nonetheless worried about using the wrong streetcar, or wheeling their baby in a forbidden park. In 1939 the Nazis, with characteristic efficiency, replaced the self-elected Jewish community organization with its own central agency for Jews: the Jüdische Kulturvereinigung. Staffed by Jews, it administered the increasingly punitive decrees affecting Jews: confiscating money, clothing, and household goods, and eventually calling up those chosen for deportation.

"The life and work here would be quite bearable," said the postcard from Birkenau, "if only the chimneys were not in our neighborhood."

Jewish children, too, could not escape the slowly closing vise. In 1938 they were barred from the public schools and restricted to those improvised by the Jewish community. With the coming of the war—when Jewish children as young as thirteen were drafted for forced labor in factories—the community ran classes for them from 5:00 to 8:00 P.M., but in October, 1941, even this instruction was forbidden. Zionist youth organizations, which had been able to maintain themselves under the camouflage of "vocational training groups," were also declared illegal. Rather than disband, they decided to continue underground, dividing themselves for safety into small groups of six and meeting clandestinely to carry on programs of self-education. The combined groups met for the last time in February, 1942. One of the members, looking to the future, wrote a report of that last meeting:

Although we do not know whether this letter will reach you, we write it nonetheless in the hope that one of us will survive and will then be able to transmit this to you. We live in the most difficult times. Many of us have already been carried off to Poland to meet an unknown fate.... Although it was very dangerous, we met here today wearing our white shirts concealed under our coats.... Then Comrade Erwin Tichauer stepped forward and called the names of those who have been carried off in the last months since the beginning of the deportations. As each name was called, we all answered . . . "hinneni" [Here!]. They are all among us because we are thinking of them, as we are sure they are thinking of us.

Although the deportations were conducted as inconspicuously as possible, the Nazis exerted every effort to set the Jews apart on the streets of Berlin. In early 1941 a curfew was imposed; Jews had to be at home by 8:00 P.M. in winter and 9:00 in summer. Then, in September, 1941, the Nazis ordered a return to

medieval symbolism, requiring every Jew over the age of six to wear a yellow star over his heart. In 1942 every Jewish household had to display a white Star of David on the door. Jews were not permitted to walk on streets that had government buildings on them or on the famous shopping boulevards. In the parks, they were allowed to sit only on special yellow benches; later they were not allowed in the parks at all.

Jews could buy no milk, eggs, fish, smoked goods, condensed milk, liquor, cheese, rice, cake, or white bread, and from November, 1942, no sugar or jam. The meager supplies still available to them—mostly cabbage, beets, potatoes, and coarse black bread—had to be bought between 4:00 and 5:00 P.M. The telephones of Jews were disconnected; they were not allowed to buy newspapers or to have their shoes repaired except at two specially designated centers. Having been forced out of their jobs, they were required to register with a special Nazi labor office. Prisoners in everything but name, they worked where they were assigned, for whatever hours their employer required, accepting whatever pay he offered. And unless they lived more than five kilometers from their place of work, they were not permitted to use a streetcar to get there.

Such regulations crowded the Jews closer to the edge of existence, taxing their strength and cutting them off from the rest of the world. But they could have endured all that, as one witness wrote, "if only there had been no transports." On October 10, 1941, the Nazis started their first call-up of Jews to be sent to concentration camps in Poland. At first the Berlin Jews accepted the Nazi story that these were organized for the purpose of "orderly resettlement in the east." Some, not wanting to be separated, even volun-

teered to go along with those who had been summoned.

Those who left in the first transports signed and sent back preprinted postcards. These scrawls were the only sign received by anxious relatives who themselves were permitted to write only one postcard a month in reply. Frau Neubauer recalled how she once threaded into a postcard yarn of many colors so that her sister would have thread, "in case she needed to darn her stockings." Very soon postcards from the east arrived only occasionally, and the cryptic messages that reached Berlin began to stir terrible doubts about the fate of those being "resettled." One young Zionist, Jizchak Schwersenz, who went underground in 1942, told of receiving a postcard in July, 1943, from Birkenau, one of the smaller camps. "The life and work here would be quite bearable," wrote his friend, "if only the chimneys were not in our neighborhood. . . . Many of us are already with Alfred." The word "chimney" had been written in Hebrew and Alfred was the leader of their Zionist group who had been shot six months earlier. The meaning of such a message, Schwersenz commented, was "unmistakable": the summons for transport was nothing less than an invitation to death. "Resettlement" simply meant murder.

Even so, the decision to go underground was not an easy one to make. The numerous papers required by the Nazis—cards of identity, forms for work, for living accommodations, for food, for clothing, for travel, even forms for receiving mail—seriously complicated any attempt to disappear. At first many Jews found it unthinkable to use false papers. Schwersenz reports that when he first contemplated the idea he found it repugnant. It seemed "impossible to me as a German brought up to standards of Prussian correctness." A fellow member of the Zionist movement finally persuaded him that "it was our duty not to permit ourselves to be slaughtered like cattle by the Nazis." In July, 1942, when his father was called up for deportation, Schwersenz tried to get him to resist. But his father, who had served in the German army in World War I, could not imagine that "the country for which he had volunteered his life would take it from him"—an attitude, Schwersenz adds, widely held in the Jewish community.

Most of those who went underground simply hid, hoping they would be able to cover their own tracks. But others relied on the help of friends. When one Jewish businessman decided to "disappear" so as to spare his Christian wife involvement in his fate, his mother-in-law found him a place to live. She telephoned a Gentile friend of hers whose son, she knew, had an office in downtown Berlin that he used infrequently. The woman who came to clean the office once a week was also in on the secret. There were, therefore, at least four people, besides his wife, who knew where this man was hiding; for all of them it was a heavy and dangerous burden.

Children not yet listed in the Nazis' central card catalogue were perhaps the easiest to hide. One teen-ager, entrusted to some Gentile friends when her parents were deported, stopped going to school and simply lived hidden away in her friends' apartment. The key to her survival lay in the perfect quietness of her life. Of all her family, which had lived in Berlin for seven generations, she alone lived through the war.

Patience is not a dramatic virtue. Yet for many of those hidden away in attics or cellars, a stubborn acceptance of monotony saved their lives. "I could not have lasted if I had known it would be two years," said Hans Rosenthal, today one of Germany's most popular television stars. Like other Jewish teen-agers, he had been drafted for forced labor. In 1943 he heard that the Pomeranian tin factory where he worked was to be closed, and fearing deportation, he decided to slip away to Berlin. There a Gentile friend of his mother's took him in and hid him in a tool shed. "I thought it would be for a few months," he said, but the few months turned into years. To pass the time he listened to the radio, read the newspaper down to the last scrap of print, and kept a wall map that he marked with troop movements and battle positions. Gradually, the neighbors became aware of his presence and some shared rations with him. The householders on the street, who had built a communal air-raid shelter, invited him in when the massive bombing raids came—welcomed him in fact. (The reason, he learned with astonishment, was a widespread superstition that no bomb would fall where a Jew was hidden.) The hours he spent in the shelter, he said, were his happiest. Only then was he free of the terrible dread that the Gestapo might come for him.

As the confusion of the war increased and bombs destroyed houses, streets, and records and put thousands of people to flight, it became more and more possible to have "lost" one's papers, and thus to claim a new identity. Some Jews with sufficient boldness and presence of mind used the opportunity to come out of hiding and blend in with the other refugees.

One such person was Ilselotte Themal, a young woman who had been hidden by Gentile friends in Berlin and who suffered under the knowledge that every day she was endangering their lives. When she heard that large parts of Hamburg, including registry offices, had been destroyed, she saw an opportunity to acquire new identity papers supposedly replacing a destroyed set. She was able to get a new set and permission to travel to West Prussia. There, her friends from Berlin who had traveled with her introduced her as a bombing victim. Her arrival in the town of a thousand people was noticed by the Polish partisans, who were then operating in the neighborhood as the eastern front moved toward Berlin. Their leader flatly accused her of being a Nazi spy. In one second she had to decide whether she could trust this stranger. "The partisans," she said, "searched deep into every newcomer's soul, and I had no recourse other than to confess the truth." Fortunately, one of her Berlin friends corroborated the story. The partisan leader accepted her word and announced: "Very well. You now stand under our protection. Nothing will happen to you." He asked if she would work for them, and this gentle young woman suddenly became a spy for the partisans.

Many of those who survived in Berlin found themselves doing things that surprised them. Yet they held on to their own ways. Frau Neubauer, married to a Christian and hence enjoying a precariously "protected" status, told me she was always careful to avoid trouble. Nonetheless, a neighbor denounced her for insulting Hitler. When the police arrived in the middle of the afternoon, Frau Neubauer had just put a plum tart in the oven. Her first thought was not her arrest but her plum tart. Standing at the door, she asked for permission to go back to the kitchen and turn off the oven. The police officer replied that she could do so if she promised not to try to escape. Offended by his mistrustful attitude and taking it as an aspersion on her

---

"Then Comrade Erwin Tichauer stepped forward and called the names of those who have been carried off in the last months since the beginning of the deportations. As each name was called, we all answered . . . 'Here!'"

**"I am more afraid today when I go home from the
theatre at night than I was when I kept
a rendezvous with the partisans in the forest."**

integrity, Frau Neubauer replied: "In that case, let it burn, and you can take me away." She spent several months in a Berlin prison. One day, for no apparent reason, she was released and allowed to return home.

Another young Jewish woman, Vera Edel, had been living out the war in Berlin with three young children. She had no papers or ration books and was desperate for food. In March, 1945, she decided to venture into the no man's land that lay on the outskirts of Berlin between the advancing Russian armies and the retreating Germans. She hoped that the farmers, fleeing the Russians, might have left some food behind. "I had long since lost my identity," she told me. "I no longer existed for any German official. It was only chance, in fact, that had kept me from being consumed in some gas oven. . . . I had to decide to take this risk rather than watch my children starve." She had prepared a complicated story, so absurd that it bore the ring of truth: Somewhere in the country was a "grandmother" who had been keeping some baby clothes for her. Since the grandmother's house was now threatened by the Russians, she had hastened to retrieve the baby clothes, and the grandmother had, of course, added a few sacks of beans. This was the story she planned to use if she was stopped by soldiers. Carrying some clothes in a knapsack, she ventured out.

For a while her luck held. When her train arrived at the village closest to the front, she left unnoticed by getting out on the side away from the platform. Then she struck out across a field toward a cluster of houses. Only when she got close did she see that they were occupied by German troops, one of whom stood waiting for her. Earnestly she told him her story. He took her to his sergeant, who not only listened sympathetically but also invited her to an Easter

dinner that was being given at the house that night. He explained that she would accompany an officer of the unit, a doctor who did not have a dinner partner. Later she would be given traveling papers and permitted to return to Berlin.

While the prospect of a real meal was a pleasure not to be dismissed lightly, an evening in the company of army officers was a highly unsettling thought. As it turned out, the doctor did not appear until nearly the end of dinner, and the other couples were so engrossed with one another that they hardly noticed her. At one point, in fact, she slipped away to the library, found a French novel that she was familiar with, settled into a chair, and with great contentment began to read. She did not realize that her intended dinner partner was already sitting in a corner of the room. After a while he spoke. "You read fast," he said pleasantly, leaning over her chair. But then, without warning, he challenged her story. Who was she really? For a long moment she contemplated the doctor and her situation, and decided that the truth was the only possible salvation. As she described the daily terror of her life, her habitual composure failed her, and she broke down. The doctor proved both discreet and sympathetic. He arranged a bed for her in the library, covered her with his own fur-lined coat, and next morning drove her to the station in his chauffeured car. On the platform, though curt and distant, he ordered his chauffeur to give her two large sacks filled with provisions.

As we sat talking in a café on the Kurfürstendamm, Ilselotte Themal recalled that those who helped Jews during the war knew that if they were caught they would meet the same fate as the Jews they were protecting. Yet today, she said, it makes her uncomfortable when

Berliners are too quick to volunteer information about what they did during the Hitler years to help Jews. Everyone who lived through that period feels a need to explain himself, and a legacy of darkness hangs over many lives.

After February, 1943, when Berlin was supposed to be *Judenrein*—purified of Jews—every Jew who lived in Berlin was either in hiding or using false papers. Where Jews lived together, they shared everything—coal, food, clothing. Needing one another so desperately, they lived carefully, and angry words were a luxury not to be indulged. But Ilselotte Themal recalls that on May 8, 1945, when Berlin was liberated by the Allies, she and her friends quarreled and shouted at one another as they had not during all their trials, and as they never would again. Until that moment, every act and every emotion had had to be measured, and there had been no way to express the simple grievances that are part of ordinary life.

These Berliners remember the war years from a distance verging on disbelief. They find it difficult to recall the old dangers. "I am more afraid today," one Jewish survivor told me, "when I go home from the theatre at night than I was when I kept a rendezvous with the partisans in the forest." They had not started out as heroes and they did not become saints. Yet they are heroes to us because they fought against a powerful and cruel machine and outwitted it. "Life goes forward," said Frau Neubauer, and during World War II she and her fellow survivors had been determined to go with it, no matter what the cost. They were no more than human, but neither were they less. In a world that had created beasts, theirs was no small achievement. □

Ruth Gay is the author of a book about Jewish life in America, published in 1965.

Torah scrolls and prayer shawls, confiscated by the Nazis and intended to be destroyed, were discovered intact in this Berlin cellar in 1946.

What to Say to the Space Probe When It Arrives

The moment may be at hand, so we ought to devise an intergalactic vocabulary

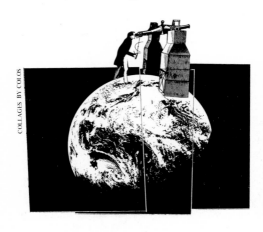

Men have long speculated about the possibility of extraterrestrial life. As early as 1686, in a work entitled *Plurality of Worlds*, Bernard de Fontenelle offered arguments in favor of the idea. A century later Alexander Copland presented both the pros and cons of the issue in *The Existence of Other Worlds: Peopled with Living and Intelligent Beings*. At the turn of our own century Percival Lowell, founder of the Lowell Observatory at Flagstaff, Arizona, argued that there were irrigation canals and oases on Mars. For several decades Lowell's theory gave rise to speculations about intelligent life on Mars.* But the findings of *Mariner 9* and *Viking 1* and *2* have put an end to the idea of technologically advanced Martians. As a result, our search for extraterrestrial civilizations has shifted away from our own solar system to distant stars—a disappointment, perhaps, but nonetheless a clear step forward.

One might suppose that as more and more facts accumulated about our space environment, thus restricting the free play of imagination, enthusiasm for the notion of extraterrestrial life might diminish. But, it has not worked out that way. On the contrary, as knowledge of astronomy has expanded over the past twenty years, so also has responsible opinion in favor of the probability of extraterrestrial life. In 1975, for example, a sober report, *The Possibility of In-*

*See "Of Mars, Martians, and *Mariner 9*," HORIZON, Summer, 1973.

telligent Life Elsewhere in the Universe, was published by the House Committee on Science and Technology. It began with this arresting sentence: "The age-old concept that man is alone in the universe is gradually fading out."

Increasingly, scientific attention is turning to the problems of communicating with extraterrestrial life. How do we get in touch with it? By what means is it most likely to try to get in touch with us? What message should we send? What questions should we ask? Some responsible thinkers, it should be noted, include only one concern: How do we keep extraterrestrial life from finding out about us in the first place?

An important reason for the increased interest in these practical matters is that we have now begun to suspect that there are many more planets—that is, potential homes for life—in space than we once thought. At first glance it might seem reasonable to suppose that if

our sun has planets, then similar suns will, too. For a long time, however, astronomers gave little credence to that argument. Most of them thought the configuration of our solar system was most plausibly explained by the so-called collision hypothesis. According to this view, the planets were formed by the tidal attraction of a star that once grazed the sun, pulling immense quantities of solar material out into space. Upon collapsing, this material became fragments circling the sun, and the fragments then condensed into the planets and their satellites.

If the collision hypothesis is correct, the presence of life outside our solar system is extremely unlikely. Because stars are so small compared to the distances separating them, collisions—and even near collisions—would seldom occur. Thus planetary systems, and a fortiori planetary life, would be correspondingly rare. As time passed, however, reasoning of a quite different kind helped tilt the interest of astronomers toward another theory. That was the venerable nebular hypothesis, formulated two centuries ago by Immanuel Kant and Marquis de Laplace. It holds that the sun condensed from a primordial nebula or cloud. Long subject to serious objections, the hypothesis has been supported by recent discoveries, among them the fact that magnetic and not just gravitational forces have played

By RONALD BRACEWELL

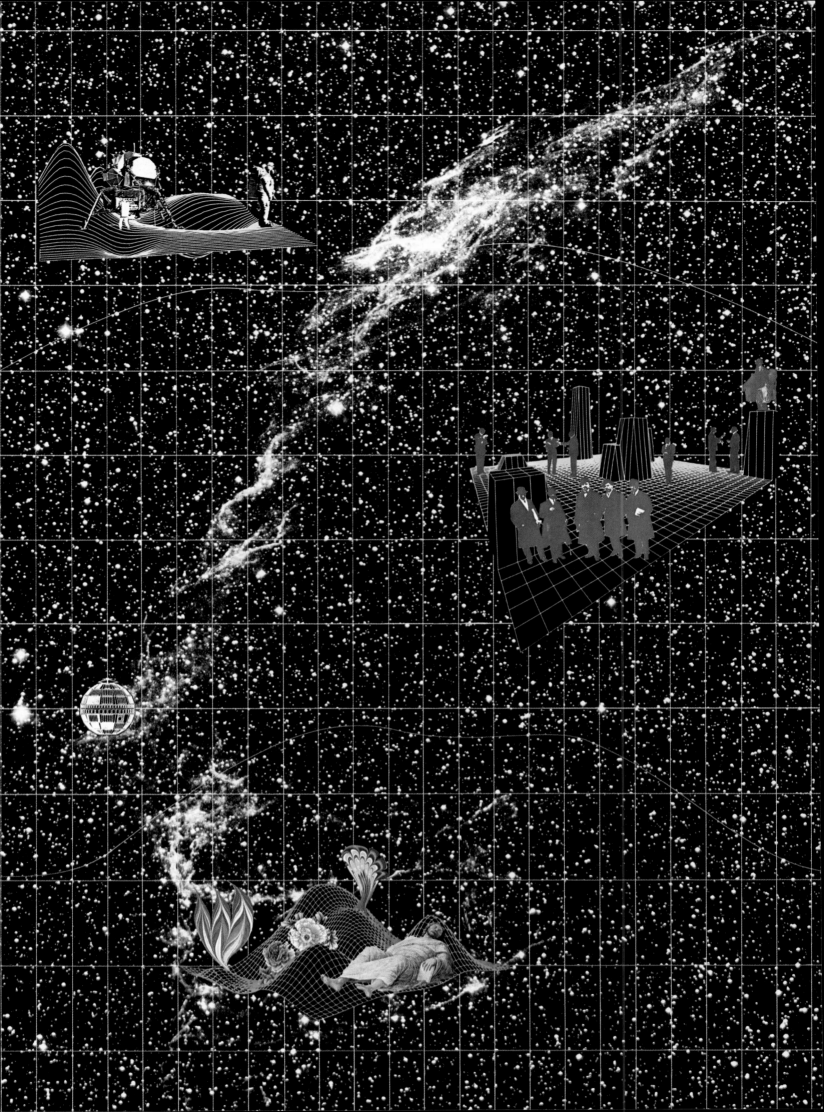

essential roles in shaping our planetary system. The clear corollary is that planets are probably quite common around other stars.

NASA is currently supporting a study aimed at finding out which nearby stars do in fact have planets. And an increasing number of scientists, both in observatories and in universities, are giving attention to other preliminaries. It is now fairly well agreed, for example, that if we are to communicate with other worlds, then electromagnetic waves will be the medium of communication, and the microwave radio band is where the activity will be, since that band offers the greatest range. There is, in fact, nothing to prevent microwave transmission to the far reaches of the galaxy; our radio telescopes routinely receive natural signals emitted tens of millenniums ago from remote celestial bodies. But even if we agree that microwave radio signals are the best means of communicating with extraterrestrial life, a crucial question remains: Should we begin the proceedings by transmitting a message or by listening for one?

Here, I think, the Columbus principle is useful. The Columbus principle says simply that explorers usually discover less-advanced peoples: if the Indians

had been more advanced in shipbuilding than the Europeans, they would have discovered Europe. I would therefore expect the initiative to be taken by the nearest community that is more advanced in space technology than we are. If there are a good many technological communities out there, some are unquestionably less advanced and some more advanced—no doubt considerably more advanced. When we look at the accelerating pace with which technology develops, we see that a community that reached our current level of development centuries or millenniums ago would probably be very able indeed.

Where might the nearest such community be? It has been argued that it may be not much more than ten light-years away. That seems unlikely to me. Such proximity, unless it had come about by pure accident, would imply an improbably great population density in space. After all, even if nearly every star had life around it, some would have only primitive life, some would be in phases analogous to our Age of Fishes or Age of Reptiles, and others would be in their Stone Age. Only a fraction would be in the age of technology, with the ability to communicate by radio and to launch space probes. Even if we take the most

optimistic possible view of things, the nearest superior community would probably be no closer than one hundred light-years away.

In 1960 Dr. Frank Drake of the National Radio Astronomy Observatory made the first attempt to receive intelligent signals from two nearby stars, Epsilon Eridani and Tau Ceti, which are eleven and twelve light-years away, respectively. The same attempt has been made by others but, needless to say, has so far not succeeded. Some people, arguing that such attempts are premature, say it is improbable that a civilization a mere ten light-years away would be sending us signals. On the other hand, it might have picked up the first signs of modern technological life on Earth when our radio transmissions began to reach it some years ago. Our television and radio transmission, much of it having leaked into space, now fills a vast sphere tens of light-years in radius. Any eavesdropper is free to listen to it. If that is what happened, members of this civilization might well want to let us know they're out there.

What should we expect them to say to us, these creatures near Epsilon Eridani, Tau Ceti, or some other star? To start with, they could not be sure we would pick up the beginning of a message. Therefore they would probably design a message that would make sense no matter where we started, perhaps in much the way a serialized magazine story incorporates a synopsis from time to time. Or they might send messages within messages, thereby providing something for everybody, including much repetition in case a listener tuned in late.

Before considering in more detail what messages might—or should—go back and forth, we need to take into account a fundamental impediment to interstellar communication: the time required for a round-trip message. An exchange over ten light-years would require twenty years, and that is the

minimum for interstellar communication. There is a risk, therefore, that twenty years or more of material would be wasted if we were to reply thoughtlessly. Thus if Earth, detecting a message from a star ten light-years away, responded, "Roger, we hear you," or the equivalent, another twenty years of the repetitious, general-purpose contact message would keep coming before we could expect any response to our response. Without some rapid exchange to set up essential housekeeping conventions such as what wavelength to use, what time schedule to keep, what language to use, what to talk about, and what technical standards to adhere to, communication might simply not get started. This is why I believe we should be prepared for the arrival of an envoy or messenger in the form of an automatically operated space vehicle.

What, exactly, may we expect from such a probe? Its primary goal will probably be to find out whether technological life is present on Earth. I avoid the term "intelligent life" because it does not necessarily imply technology. On our own planet, technology probably developed because in prehistoric times human intelligence was honed on warfare, and a premium was placed on cunning and weaponry. Much the same pattern would surely prevail elsewhere. That is not to say that some gentle Buddha could not have influenced whole populations to follow quite different, less competitive paths. But if our own history is any guide, such a population would have been overrun by those who value technical mastery of nature. Technological life, rather than merely intelligent life, is what will determine membership in the galactic communication network.

An automatic probe from another galaxy, using a simple radio receiver, could easily ascertain that powerful television transmitters and defense radars are in use on Earth and that technological life is absent from the other

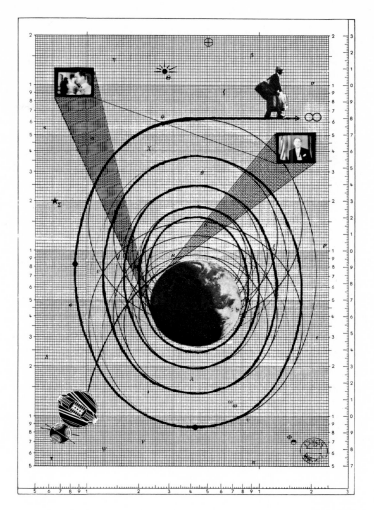

planets in our solar system. The visiting probe will duly note this discovery and report its findings back to its home planet, where a receiving installation will be monitoring reports from this and other probes. (Most probes will not encounter advanced life, and in such cases they will merely send back physical data and photographs, just as our probes to our own planets do now.) But when an Earth probe hits the jackpot, it will try, I imagine, to attract our attention.

This will not be difficult. All the probe will need to do is emit signals on wavelengths already in use on Earth—a virtual guarantee that some audience somewhere will be tuned to those wavelengths. It is true that the audience first receiving such a signal might ignore it or perceive it as minor interference and tune to some other program. But as soon as the probe begins interfering with some important activity—the Channel 5 news, let's say, or a coastal defense

radar system—it will get plenty of attention. Within hours its position in interplanetary space will be pinpointed and its orbit worked out.

What then? For example, what about the legal aspects of extraterrestrial contact? Which government agencies should be alerted? Who should determine the content of any response we might send? What would be the role of other sovereign powers and of the United Nations? No worldwide, practical planning has been done. If, for example, an amateur radio operator picked up the first message tomorrow, word would quickly spread around the world and there would be little chance of responsible organization.

Furthermore, such contact might even be dangerous for our civilization. Professor George Wald, the distinguished Harvard Nobelist, has warned that "danger lurks in the stars," and astronomer Ždenek Kopal has said, "For

We will not decide simply to hunker down and act as if we aren't here. . . . What might our message be?

God's sake, let us not answer." On this subject the House report says:

Since we have no knowledge of their nature, we may be aiding in our own doom. Although it is tempting to assume that any civilization advanced enough to travel over interstellar space would have overcome the petty differences that cause wars, they may not be sure if we have. They may have encountered other warlike peoples and learned . . . to arrive . . . ready for combat.

Such fears need to be openly discussed and our position determined in advance. Personally, I find it hard to imagine much of any threat, particularly of a familiar kind, emanating from the immense interstellar distances. I will therefore assume that we will not decide simply to hunker down and act as if we aren't here. After all, the probe already knows we are here and has already sent a message to that effect to its home base. We shall not be able to conceal our existence at that point.

The messenger probe, not yet knowing that we know it is there, must continue to broadcast until it receives an acknowledgment. What form should our acknowledgment take? One thing we could do is abruptly change, or terminate, transmission, as a signal that sentient beings are down here and are ready for its message.

Before communication can occur, a number of technical matters will have to be settled—first, perhaps, the hours of transmission. Earth can hardly listen in and send replies twenty-four hours a day. A base on the ground can transmit only to points above the horizon, and as Earth spins on its axis the probe may sink below the horizon. In time we can easily arrange for round-the-clock receiving and transmitting, perhaps by launching a satellite that transmits everywhere in space except for the relatively narrow shadow regions lying behind the sun, moon, and Earth itself. At first, however, scheduling will be crucial, and not only because of such technical limitations. For all the probe knows at the beginning of our dialogue, Earth might have meteorological phenomena like the global sandstorms of Mars, or thunderstorms that interrupt radio communication (as indeed do occur throughout the humid tropics on many afternoons). For the probe to ignore such phenomena would be to risk wasting parts of its message, and it would surely be programmed to deal with interruptions. One way for us to help prepare for this necessity will be to use signals meaning "hello," "uh-huh," and "bye-bye." We will teach the probe these signals by starting a session with

"hello," ending it with "bye-bye," and making frequent use of the acknowledging "uh-huh" in between. In the case of telephone calls, such trifles strike us more as conventional courtesies than as essential elements of information transfer. Where space conversations are concerned, however, they are indispensable. Without them, each time there is an equipment breakdown at our end (or a strike or fund shortage or any other interruption) there will be a loss of message. Other technical exchanges will need to take place. Assuming all such problems are ironed out, what might our message be?

First of all, there is the question of language. Ordinary English can rather easily be decoded. Consider the archaic languages that have been deciphered, and bear in mind that we are talking here about the very opposite of cryptography: anticryptography. Cuneiform inscriptions were not, after all, composed for the benefit of the archaeologists who were later to decipher them, whereas the English text transmitted to an alien probe will, of course, be chosen specifically to make decipherment easy. We can get off to a good start by transmitting an illustrated English dictionary. Better still, I think, we can send animated cartoons by means of television. It is an amusing exercise to apply animation to anticryptography. Many words that cannot possibly be

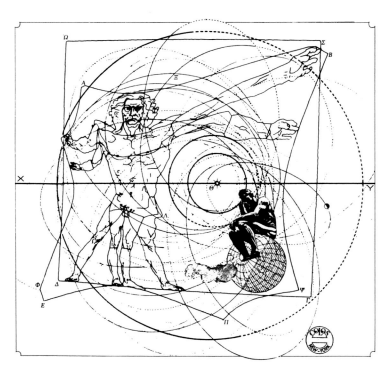

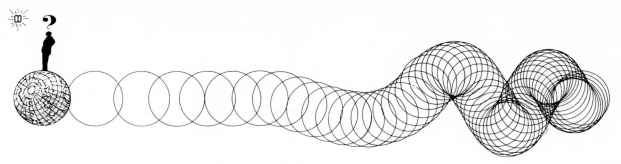

represented by a single illustration can be conveyed quite readily by animated sequences, so I expect television to be the natural medium for communication with an interstellar messenger.

Consider some of the advantages. Since the main purpose of a probe will be to agree on wavelengths, schedules, and other technical matters, the first bit of information the probe will wish to communicate is the location of the home base. The probe does not, of course, know our names for the various stars, nor does it know our systems for describing the location of an object in space. For that matter, it does not even yet know our number system.

Television neatly permits it to by-pass these problems and to exhibit to us the familiar pattern of a constellation of stars, perhaps Cygnus the Swan. Imagine the excitement in Earth's receiving station as the participants realize that this is an attempt to tell where the probe came from. In reply, the project leader takes the video tape of the constellation, threads it into the transmitter, and sends the same picture back to the probe. By this beautifully elementary maneuver the probe is informed that its opening statement has been seen. It will be a simple matter to program an automatic probe to withhold the next item until an acknowledgment is received.

As I imagine this first encounter of mankind with another culture, I see one of the stars of the Swan in the television picture begin to wink; the beginning of the precious message has been safely transferred. Then we will send our acknowledgment. After that the probe will transmit a travelogue—zooming us in on the home star and then in on the home planet. Perhaps we can reciprocate by offering scenes of the Rockies or the Oregon coast, asking whether the probe wishes to accept such material for retransmission to its home.

Probably it will not: we can transmit it ourselves, much better, once we have the wavelength and schedule. After all, we have bigger antennas and more transmitter power than would be economical to incorporate in a modest probe whose basic function is to serve as a catalyst for direct communication. Of more immediate urgency will be to get the technical details of wavelength, schedule, power level, and so on safely into our hands. After that it can relax, and we can hope that its computer memory will contain much to regale us with during the long interval before a transmission from the home base arrives.

Once the housekeeping details are out of the way, what should we send to the other planet? The probe may suggest some preferences of its own, but the order of priorities will not be very important in a transmission lasting decades. We could send every word of several encyclopedias, textbooks in the principal fields of knowledge, and selections from world literature. All viewpoints could be accommodated. Lewis Thomas, in *The Lives of a Cell*, says:

Perhaps the safest thing to do at the outset, if technology permits, is to send music. . . . I would vote for Bach, all of Bach, streamed out into space, over and over again. We would be bragging, of course, but it is surely excusable for us to put the best possible face on at the beginning of such an acquaintance.

Since round-trip message times might be a couple of centuries, our natural impatience to get on with the job had best be tempered with some mature reflection. After all, the interval between a question and its reply would exceed the human life span. Interstellar communication must therefore be between long-lived societies rather than between things as ephemeral as individuals, governments, or nations. (How many two-hundred-year-old nations are there?)

Once the long-term character of interstellar communication is appreciated, it does not seem unreasonable to accept delays of even thousands of years. The things we might learn would no doubt be worth waiting for.

To start with, we shall undoubtedly want to include a sort of shopping list in our message—things we need to find out. A number of our serious problems today depend heavily on science or technology for their solution. The energy crisis, for example, would be alleviated if we knew how to produce clean nuclear energy. The population problem, the food crisis, the problem of cancer and other diseases—all these things depend partly for their solution upon science. Or consider our international political problems. It would be of great value to have before us the detailed example of another world where global political stability existed. It is possible, of course, that another culture will have nothing to offer toward the solution of such problems. On the other hand, it might have much to offer.

If a steady stream of new information and new science began to flow into our society—discoveries we could not have hoped to make on our own for years—the consequences could not help but be beneficial. Most significantly, we would be drawn into the mainstream of a vast galactic culture. For when, finally, we begin to communicate with some distant culture, it is extremely unlikely that it will be the first such occurrence anywhere. Then the really significant conversations will at last begin—conversations about what we, and they, value most; about whom we, and they, most admire and respect; and, perhaps most important of all, about the meaning of life, wherever it may be found. □

Ronald Bracewell of Stanford University is the author of The Galactic Club.

Krishna:
God as a Troublesome Youth

Though the news may shock his modern adherents, Lord Krishna was not a nice boy

The Western world began to hear of Krishna a few years ago when the man in the street, walking down that street of his in New York, London, Paris, and Rome, met young men and women curiously attired in robes unsuitable to the climate, dancing a simple dance to even simpler songs and behaving with childlike happiness.

The man in the street may have assumed that these cavorting youths were part of the current drug culture, but, as it turned out, the youngsters were forbidden to touch even tea and coffee, much less drugs. And to anybody who took the trouble to ask, they replied that they were happy because they were in love with an Indian boy called Krishna.

A few inquiring persons, including myself, who looked closely at the Krishna Consciousness movement found that it was every bit as innocent as its adherents said it was. Indeed, the sect is so harmless and happy that I rather hope none of its devotees will read what follows, which is the true story of Govinda the cowherd, otherwise known as Lord Krishna.

We owe the story of Krishna the cowherd to a group of Indian pastoral nomads—the Abhiras—who, as sometimes happens with people living off the

In Brooklyn, New York, two devotees of Krishna Consciousness, above, celebrate their marriage, in which sexual continence will be the rule. In a detail, opposite, from an eighteenth-century Indian miniature, the god Krishna embraces his favorite paramour, Radha.

land, had highly independent views of their own. They lived in about the first century A.D. in a territory named Braj along the river Jumna in northern India. Braj, with its beautiful forest, is as holy to many Indians as Jerusalem is to Christians, for devotees of Krishna believe that he actually lived there. He may well have, and if he did, he was certainly what the Irish call a broth of a boy. He was a naughty baby, a mischievous lad, and a totally immoral young man, a Don Juan who delighted in breaking up the peace of well-regulated families. He was, as a result, worshiped as a god and, as we all know, he still is.

The story of Krishna began because the Abhiras apparently felt exasperated

with the orderly life, the comfortable round. They had reason to be bored. The Hindu civilization around them was at its self-satisfied height. There was prosperity. There was a stable society in which everybody knew his or her place and, because of the caste system, stayed in it. Religion was as important to the Hindus as it is to the pope in the Vatican, and just as well organized. Better organized, in fact, because there were no rebel priests or trendy theologians. One worshiped Vishnu or Shiva. Daily life, from the cradle to the pyre, was centered around what we nowadays call the extended family: mother and father, children, old folks, and relatives. Sometimes the family was considerably extended, because a man could have more than one wife.

Morality consisted in preserving this family and supporting the highest caste of all, the Brahmans, who had an answer for everything. They were the marriage counselors, the psychiatrists, the sociologists, the clergymen, and the educators of the time, except that they did not have to talk so much. They had little need to: every good Hindu knew that he paid for the sins he had committed in his previous incarnations, and he would pay for any new sins in his next

ALL: NATIONAL MUSEUM, NEW DELHI—RAGHUBIR SINGH

According to Hindu legend, Krishna, the principal avatar of the god Vishnu, spent his youth among the cowherds of Braj, a region of northern India, where he was beset by jealous gods and the evil demon Kansa. A giant crane, left, sent by Kansa, has tried to swallow Krishna, but Krishna, center, emerges from the crane's throat, splits his massive beak, and kills him.

Agni, the god of fire, resents the cowherds' love of Krishna and causes a forest fire, which Krishna quenches by sucking the flames into his mouth.

Krishna, center, finally dispatches Kansa by dashing the demon's body to the ground; above, Krishna's half brother Balarama attacks Kansa's brothers.

one. The principal sin, it should be noted, was to disobey the Brahmans.

Into these placid waters the Abhiras flung Krishna. Shortly after he was born he was rescued, by stratagem, from a monarch who, like Herod, ordered the slaughter of babies because of a prophecy. But Krishna's resemblance to Jesus ends there: Jesus was the model of what a good boy should be, while Krishna played every trick on his parents that he could think of. He was a habitual thief, much given to stealing curds, a delicacy of the times. To stop him, his mother would tie him to a tree or to a large rock, but to no avail. Either the rope would magically lengthen or a devoted playmate would give him another one, and he would get his curds. The child, grinning as happily as little Jack Horner and eating his booty, is a favorite subject of popular pictures sold everywhere in India, displayed by hucksters on the dirt roads of villages or, in cities, on the pavement. In my own family house there was a much-prized rendition in repoussé silver of Krishna eating curds. Although I was told the story, I was not told that another of Krishna's tricks was to urinate on the floor of any house he did not take a fancy to.

Now I would ask the Western reader who wishes to follow me into the Hindu mind to reflect that two added to two makes four; or, to contemplate the fact that the letter *c*, followed by *a*, and concluded by *t*, spells *cat*. It has cost, I am sure, no great effort. In the same way, the Hindu has grasped the fact that we are born, we grow, we go through a stage known as adolescence, we feel various urges, known as sex, after which we become an adult. For some years as an adult we are not very wise, but because we are young, we enjoy ourselves, with no very good reason except that we are young and (just barely) adult.

The Hindu has always accepted this process as the West accepts night and day. Of course, the process goes on: we mature, we age, we die. Of this latter business, the Hindu is as much bedeviled with doubts and puzzles as any Westerner and is quite as full of unsatisfactory explanations. But in the matter of growing up—in the matter of sex—he can be quite irritatingly untroubled. Krishna embodies this unique calm. He is the god of common sense about youth. He steals the bread out of the mouths of our psychologists, with the aplomb he showed stealing the curds.

At the heart of Krishna worship is an admiration for his lusty, carefree adolescence, a period that we should think of as extending beyond the teens into the early twenties. His love life is celebrated not only in religious texts but also in some of the most beautiful poems in Indian literature. The story is told in a great number of them; the one I shall follow is that beloved by millions of Indians. It was written by the poet Nanddas in the sixteenth century. The poet died about 1585, ten years before Shakespeare wrote *Romeo and Juliet*, another celebration of young love. Nanddas's poem is in Hindi but is based on a Sanskrit text. It is called *The Round Dance of Krishna*. Krishna does not in fact dance, but the girls do. Indeed, you can see the girls dancing for love of Krishna even today, just as you can see Romeo wooing Juliet. There is one important difference: in the love story of Krishna there are no Montagues and Capulets to trouble the waters. It is all as simple as two and two makes four.

We are by the river Jumna, which flows past the Taj Mahal. There are pastures and a forest. The forest is Indian; that is, it has rather small trees, many glades, and a profusion of flowering bushes. It is called Vrindāvan, a name that to Indian ears has the same magic as Eden has to ours, but without all that fuss about the apple.

Krishna is a cowherd. He is, I suppose, about eighteen and he is the handsomest lad in the village. The girls also look after the cattle, but with only a part of their attention. Krishna plays the flute, and when he plays it the girls go out of their minds with love, in just the same way they fall for a pop idol today.

All the girls are members of good, steady families. Some of them have been betrothed to suitable partners by their parents, who, of course, only wish them well; others are already married. Krishna sounds his flute, and the girls flock to him, their bosoms heaving with desire. They should do nothing of the sort, of course. They should stay at home and think of their husbands or future husbands. But if they do, says the poet (and with him all Krishna worshipers), they will never know true love, which is by its very nature disruptive and antisocial. "Hate domesticity," the poet advises.

With just one finger Krishna holds up the mountain Govardhana in order to shelter the cowherds from a terrible rainstorm sent by the god Indra. Krishna toys like this one are popular in India today.

The girls stream out of their houses, their anklets and bracelets making the cheerful, stamping jingle that is one of the attractions of Indian dance. They gather around the beautiful boy. He speaks lovingly to them all, for Krishna has the gift of gab.

Suddenly the girls are flung into the utmost consternation. Krishna tells them all to go home. They gaze at him, petrified. One by one they find their voices. Naturally it would be right and proper to go home before husband, or mother and father and grandma start worrying. Certainly there are the pots to be washed at home and the huts to be tidied up. But why should Krishna tell them that? They begin to sob with

disappointment, and (says the poet) Krishna is thoroughly delighted. We can see today that mother and father were right: Krishna is not a *nice* boy.

Nice or not, he is a past master at the love game. He is fully aware of a fact that George Bernard Shaw wrote an enormously long play to prove. In *Man and Superman* Don Juan learns that it is the female who chases the male, not the other way around. Krishna therefore runs away into the forest. The girls go in full cry after him. In their haste they trample down a whole catalogue of flowers, giving the poet a chance for some exquisitely beautiful verses and a sly line or two about plants that are supposed to be aphrodisiacs.

Of course, Krishna allows the girls to catch up. The place he selects is a beach, then as now (and probably always) a setting that arouses erotic thoughts. The beach is on the shores of the Jumna, and there he fondles the heated young cowherds in several explicitly named places. The girls are delighted, but at this point in the story a comic episode intervenes. Another boy appears on the scene: Kamdev, the god of love, or, as we would call him, Cupid. He promptly falls in love with Krishna. In our days this triangular situation would give writers a great opportunity for complex and heavy drama. The Hindus, who I believe to be the only people in history that have never taken homosexuality seriously, settle the matter in quick time. Cupid's wife, Rati, arrives on the beach, and carries her aberrant husband off out of the story.

Once more Krishna takes off into the forest, and the girls resume the chase. Stated baldly, the tale begins to take on the semblance of the Keystone Kops. That is because I am deprived of the poetry. The girls talk to the flowers and the trees, asking for news of their love. It is one of the most beautiful sequences in old Indian poetry, and I do not think it too much to compare it with Shelley's

TEXT CONTINUED ON PAGE 64

Leaving their sleeping husbands behind, the herdgirls of Braj cluster adoringly around Krishna.

The Dark God at Play

A PORTFOLIO OF RAJPUT PAINTINGS

Krishna plays his flute for Radha.

It is a clear autumn evening in Braj along the river Jumna; a sliver of moon lights the sky and the air is heavy with the scent of jasmine. Krishna, "the mighty prince of lovers," fulfilling a promise he once made to the herdgirls, calls them from their houses with his flute:

> A song so sweet as to bewitch the hearts
> Of the shy-eyed girls of Braj;
>
> They heard it play! and now their way
> To the melody they make,
> Young wives, impatient of delay . . .

For centuries Krishna's love affairs with the herdgirls, and especially with his favorite, Radha, have been a beloved theme of Indian painting and poetry. The charming pictures here and on the following pages were painted by artists of the Punjab Hills in the late 1700's or early 1800's, and the quoted passages are from *The Round Dance of Krishna* by the sixteenth-century poet Nanddas, as translated by the Hindi scholar Stuart McGregor.

Sitting in a tree, Krishna teases the naked herdgirls.

One day when the herdgirls are bathing in the river Jumna, Krishna steals their clothes, climbs a tree, and naughtily orders them out of the water. Trying at first to hide themselves, the girls finally emerge, saying to one another that since Krishna already knows their hearts, there is no point in being shy. When he returns their garments and goes away, they are sorely disappointed. On another occasion by the river, Krishna meets their desire with passion of his own:

> He laughs, thrills to mingling joys,
> Touches their breasts, and loins—
> Love wakes and burns, unslaked,
> As young clouds spill their rain! . . .
> And now they plunge in Jumna's stream,
> Brighter in beauty than a man can say,
> And gambol, as an elephant-king may
> Among his tender queens . . .

Krishna and the girls enjoy a moonlight swim in the river Jumna.

Distraught, the herdgirls search the forest for Krishna.

Krishna and Radha make love on a flower-strewn terrace.

Again Krishna has left the herdgirls in the forest near the river. They wander about forlornly, asking his whereabouts of the trees:

> Fair coral-tree! Brave oleander! Pray,
> Have you seen Krishna in these parts? . . .
> *Kadamba* tree! Neem! Mango! why
> This silence, for you've seen
> Him somewhere, passing by!

Presently they come upon Radha, who has also been abandoned by Krishna:

> And she stands alone, and cries
> "Dear lord whose arm is long
> To save the ones you love, what has become
> Of you? Where have you gone?"

But Krishna has not left them forever and returns to make love with them all; even when he grows older and marries some sixteen thousand wives, he always remembers them:

> And though the dark god rules
> Uncounted cosmoses as his alone,
> It's they, the assembled queens of Braj,
> Who truly grace his throne!

famous ode, in which the dejected poet speaks to the west wind and ends, immortally, "If Winter comes, can Spring be far behind?"

Here, too, the poetic invocation of nature has a climax, sad for the girls but stirring to Indian hearts down through the centuries. They finally come upon Krishna in the forest with Radha, his favorite. From our contemporary point of view, the interesting thing about Krishna and Radha is that she is another man's wife. Perhaps even more interesting to those of us who study the complexities of sex is the next scene. Krishna once more flees, and the girls, deprived of his presence, make do with Radha. They fondle her, kiss her, and lead her back to the beach by the Jumna, praising her beauty.

But it is Krishna they want, and in their burning desire for him they fall in love with the very feet that are carrying him away. In particular, they want him to place these feet on their breasts.

If only for aesthetic reasons, this love story could not consist merely of a series of frustrations. The whole poem, the entire Krishna cult, is as much an apotheosis of the successful love between the sexes as is the Song of Solomon. Inevitably Krishna reappears, and the girls fling themselves into his arms. Since there are quite a number of girls, and Krishna has only one pair of arms, this creates a problem. It is solved by a device that goes deeply into the feelings of romantic love. Krishna multiplies himself and makes love to each of the girls simultaneously, but each has the sensation that she is alone with him.

Krishna acquits himself to everyone's satisfaction, but he stands a little aside from the transports in order to give them a dab of philosophy. Whatever mysterious powers he may have (and he is, of course, a god), love, he says, is supreme, and it is in love that he finds his own happiness. When Christian missionaries in India tried to argue that this is much the same as the Sermon on the Mount, they were promptly told by Hindus that they did not know what they were talking about. In this the

Throngs of Krishna Consciousness devotees parade on Fifth Avenue in New York, above, and a lone worshiper in Trinidad pays homage, below, to a figure of the god. Krishna is worshiped throughout the world, but his youthful exploits as the carefree cowherd of Braj are best remembered by the Hindus themselves; a young boy, opposite, plays the part of Krishna at a recent festival along the Ganges.

Hindus are right, for Krishna is no ascetic. When the girls go off to bathe in the Jumna, it is clear that he watches their swinging bottoms with satisfaction.

But before they depart, they perform the Dance of the Cowgirls, one of the favorite themes of popular Indian art. Krishna plays his flute; the girls move around him, anklets jingling and hands weaving those complex gestures that every Westerner who has seen Indian

ballet will recognize, even if he does not know what they mean. So far as this particular dance is concerned, he ought not to know. The poem concludes with the warning that its meaning should not be explained to infidels. The love of Krishna is only for initiates.

Whatever the young in the West may think, Bhaktivedanta Swami Prahbhupada is a heretic. He is the founder of the Krishna Consciousness movement, whose followers dance, not around Krishna, but on our city pavements. Only the first two syllables of his name are orthodox. Bhakti is the name of a type of worship that is in rebellion against the rigidities of Brahmanic religion. It preaches that true, transcendental joy can be attained only by an ecstatic, all-embracing love of Krishna, who is seen as the supreme deity and not a mere incarnation of Vishnu. There is scant attention to ritual and formulas. The sect that worships Krishna in the bhakti manner was founded in the sixteenth century by a mystic, Chaitanya, precisely in those woods where the girls, Radha, and the god of love were consumed with a fleshly passion for the Divine Cowherd.

The sect flourishes even in modern India, and as life there grows daily more complicated and unsatisfactory (as it does for us in the West), the sect grows in strength. Needless to say, its devotees hold the Krishna Consciousness movement in amused contempt. But they do not oppose it. It will do for Westerners. It will give them at least a glimpse of what the love of Krishna really means, the love that brought Radha and the dancing cowherds a supreme happiness. And not only to them. Later texts give Krishna other love affairs, less well remembered and less well described: sixteen thousand of them, according to some sources, but that is only spoiling a rather beautiful story. The way I have told it here is the way the Hindus, probably the world's most mysterious people, know it. □

Aubrey Menen set forth his views on Hindu mystics in the Autumn, 1973, issue.

Greek Art
from the Atlantic Depths

H.M.S. *Colossus* sank in 1798
with Sir William Hamilton's Greek vases aboard.
Now the cargo—worth some $2 million—
is being salvaged, piece by precious piece

It was a July day in 1975, and even out at sea in England's hottest summer in 150 years the heat beat heavily on the surface of the water as it lapped gently against the small dory anchored a mile or so off Samson in the Scilly Isles. In the boat Mark Horobin stood upright in his black rubber suit, diver's mask in hand, head now bare, enjoying the sun after the cold on the seabed thirty feet below. Suddenly a flurry of bubbles broke the water's surface and another diver surged into the open and swam strongly toward the dory. In a trice Slim Macdonnell reached the side and, loosening a cylinder from his shoulders, bounded up the ladder and into the boat. He stretched out his hand to Mark; wet and glistening on the open palm lay a piece of pottery, a fragment from a Greek vase made more than two thousand years ago. This potsherd was conclusive proof that the ship lying scattered on the seabed below was the *Colossus*.

H.M.S. *Colossus*, once a seventy-four-gun man-of-war in Nelson's fleet, had set sail from the Mediterranean in late November, 1798. Before leaving, she had surrendered her spare anchor to Nelson's *Vanguard*, and when she ran into a fierce storm off the Scilly Isles, her remaining main anchor could not hold. On December 10 she drifted helplessly onto Southward Well, a reef of partly submerged rock just south of Samson, where she foundered and sank. She went down with the loss of only one life, but with her was lost part of a unique collection of ancient Greek vases belonging to Sir William Hamilton.

William Hamilton was born in 1730, the youngest son of Lord Archibald Hamilton and a grandson of the third duke of Hamilton. Between 1764 and 1800 he lived in Naples, serving as British minister to the court of the Two Sicilies, a position that won him distinction as a diplomat and the deep personal friendship of King Ferdinand and Queen Maria Carolina. By a sad irony of fate Hamilton is now chiefly remembered as the "husband of Nelson's Emma," but in his own day, as well as for his diplomacy, he became known throughout Europe as a music lover, patron of the arts, scholar, and connoisseur. His own words record his deep interest also in "the antiquities and natural curiosities of the country"; he reported regularly on the volcanic activity of Vesuvius to the Royal Society in London (Horace Walpole dubbed him the "Professor of Earthquakes"), while the excavations in progress at Herculaneum and Pompeii since the 1740's, which he frequently visited, awakened in him a passion for archaeology and collecting.

Within seven years of his arrival in Naples Hamilton had gathered together an important collection of classical antiquities: more than six thousand coins, three thousand other antiquities, and more than seven hundred vases. His collection was truly wide-ranging: objects of the Greek, Etruscan,

Mark Horobin, one of the team excavating the Colossus, *holds up a fragment of a fourth-century* B.C. *Greek bowl found on the seabed.*

By ANN BIRCHALL

This jumble of pottery fragments from the shipwreck has been set to dry in the sun. Mysterious bits of painted flowers, human figures, and faces, they are like pieces of a jigsaw puzzle that may, with luck, be put together again. So far some nine thousand such shards have been recovered.

and Roman periods, fashioned in gold, bronze, amber, terra cotta, glass, bone, ivory, and marble. The cream of his collection was, however, the vases. That Hamilton was judged a "vase man" even in his own day is proved by the hand-colored etching published in 1801 that caricatures him as a vase. In the Reynolds portrait dated 1777, he sits with five vases grouped around him, most prominent being the superb water jar made in Athens about 410 B.C. that may well have been the favorite vase of his early collecting days. When, impoverished by his purchases, Hamilton was obliged to sell the collection in 1772, it was acquired by the British Museum, for whom it represented a major acquisition in the general field of classical antiquities, the vases forming the nucleus of one of the finest collections of Greek vases in the world today.

When Hamilton, created knight of the Bath while he was on leave in England in 1772, returned to Naples, he

began to build up yet another collection. It was this second collection, which grew to some one thousand vases and at one time included the Portland vase, that Goethe saw during his visit to Italy in 1787; it was from these vases, too, that Emma, Sir William's second wife, whom he had married in 1791, selected her theatrical props when she performed her tableau vivant, the poses that became known as the Attitudes. Hamilton himself judged his second collection of vases "far more beautiful and complete than the series in London" when he unsuccessfully tried to sell them to the king of Prussia in 1796. But the vases, which might have gone to Berlin, were to experience quite a different fate.

An eighteenth-century man-of-war

Late in 1798, during a critical phase in the Napoleonic War, Italy faced imminent invasion by the French, and King Ferdinand ordered his court to evacuate Naples. Amidst mounting uncertainty and confusion, Hamilton's treasures were hastily packed for shipment home and part put on board H.M.S. *Colossus*. Late in December Sir William, Emma, and the Neapolitan royal family together reached safety at Palermo; but by then the *Colossus* and her precious cargo had found a watery grave on the bed of the Atlantic.

"You do me justice in thinking and knowing me to be a philosopher, but my Philosophy has been put to the Trial by the loss of the *Colossus*"—thus wrote Sir William to Charles Greville, his nephew, on learning that the ship transporting part of his unique collection had been wrecked. (It was not until the safe arrival later of the *Foudroyant* with the rest of his vases that Hamilton was at all consoled.) Owing to the circumstances

67

in which the second collection had been packed, it has never been clear what was lost with the *Colossus*. The number of vases on board was apparently never recorded, but fortunately the quality of many individual pieces had already been captured by the drawings that Wilhelm Tischbein, director of the Royal Academy of Painting at Naples, assembled in Italy and published in several folio volumes from 1791 onward. Hamilton had commissioned Tischbein to illustrate the second collection, and these elegant outline drawings were to have a profound influence on artists such as John Flaxman, one of the greatest artists of the English neoclassical movement, and to serve successive generations of classical scholars as precious substitutes for the lost originals.

As the years passed, the chances of finding the *Colossus* and of rediscovering Hamilton's vases seemed to recede. But in 1939 a diver, Roland Morris of Penzance, found his imagination fired by the story of the *Colossus* and began to search for the wreck. But it was not until the years following 1969, while diving successively on the wrecks of the *Association*, the *Romney*, and the *Eagle*—the seabed around the Scilly Isles is littered with scores of wrecked ships of different periods—that Morris, Slim Macdonnell, Mark Horobin, and Mike Hicks were able to begin a systematic search, combining underwater exploration with painstaking research into contemporary accounts of the wrecking. By August, 1974, patience and perseverance brought their reward; the team had located a battered wreck off Southward Well, accumulated sufficient evidence to identify it as that of an eighteenth-century man-of-war, and concluded that it was the *Colossus*. Under the Protection of Wrecks Act of 1973, the English law protecting the wreck sites of ancient ships, the wreck area was designated a protected site solely on the grounds of the historical and archaeological importance of the cargo—Hamilton's collection. In the spring of 1975 the team was granted the exclusive license, under my archaeological direction, first to survey

1. Clearing the seabed of kelp

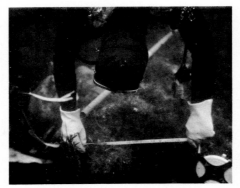

2. Laying down the grid

3. Shards soaking in a water table

4. Diver Roland Morris and Ann Birchall

Underwater excavation, properly done, is a rigorous and painstaking task. The Colossus *lies in murky water, thick with kelp. Divers cut it down, above (1), before laying out a grid of one-meter squares marked by line and poles (2). Next they sift the sand in each square at least twice, and any shards they find are labeled according to "findspot" and then taken ashore. Each batch of fragments is bathed for some four hundred hours in running water (3) to rid them of sea salt. Then, at last, the work of reassembling them begins (4).*

the site and then, after the finding of the first Greek potsherd, to excavate it.

The divers' first task was to clear the area for excavation by removing a forest of weed: tough, densely packed stems of broad-bladed kelp up to two meters long and with holdfasts like tree roots; this was hacked down with knives and brought in bundles to the surface to be borne away on the tide. Then, using a nonfloating, nonstretch fluorescent line, a grid was laid out: two ten-meter squares, designated as A and B, and each further subdivided into one-meter squares, numbered 1 to 100. The aim of the excavation was the systematic clearance of the site by working across the grid, meter square by meter square: where necessary, huge boulders of rock were lifted out of the way by a canvas air-bag, then the sand was drawn aside, sometimes by the use of an air-powered sand-probe, sometimes by a gasoline-driven water jet. Once cleared of weed and boulders, each square was carefully searched. Visibility was often a problem for the divers, so they tried to work as far away from each other as possible and developed a method of controlled movements of the hand to fan sand gently away. "Surface" finds, like the very first, might be spotted on a clean patch of sand or rock, to be collected by eager fingers, but experience taught that for every shard lying exposed on the seabed dozens more lay buried in the sand below. The sand and silt of every square was sifted at least twice so that not even the tiniest scrap of pottery would be missed. Packed into rigid polyethylene containers and labeled as each was filled, the shards were lifted into the boat waiting above. For six weeks the divers worked, until the season was closed by September's southeasterly winds. By then the total number of fragments of Greek pottery found had passed the eight-thousand mark.

In a temporary laboratory set up in Penzance by Roland Morris, the shards received conservation treatment under the advice of Mr. Harold Barker, keeper of the conservation department at the British Museum. In batches corre-

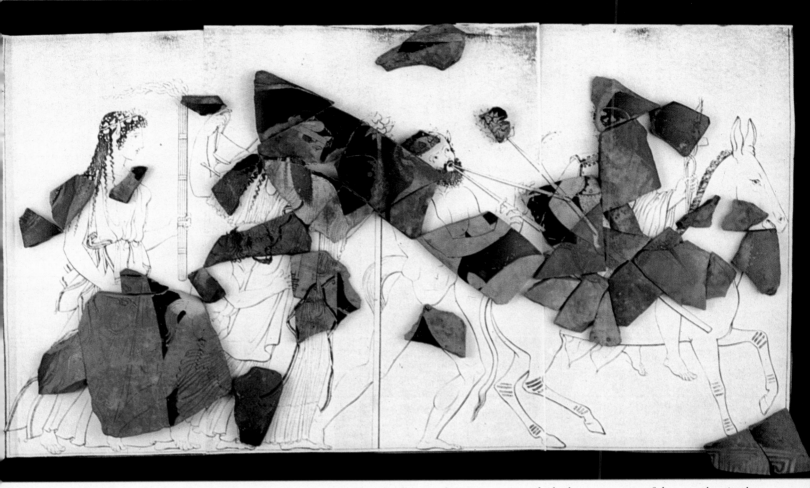

Some twenty-nine fragments of a bell krater—a bowl for mixing wine—made around 440 B.C. are matched, above, to a copy of the 1771 drawing by Wilhelm Tischbein of the painting on the krater. Emerging from the fragments is a lively scene of revelry with the Greek gods Dionysus and Hephaestus.

sponding to the grid squares in which they had been excavated, the fragments were spread out—a dazzling, breathtaking array—in specially constructed "water tables," long shallow tanks built of marine ply, into which fresh water cascaded at one end, flowed gently through, and drained away at the other. Thus constantly changing water washed over the pottery fragments, gradually soaking away the soluble salts from nearly two centuries' immersion in the sea. The shards were then spread on tables to dry in a warm atmosphere. It was in the laboratory that we were able to appreciate for the first time not only the overall quantity of the fragments but also their relative density as discovered in the various squares of our underwater grid. Some of the squares, such as A 12, seemed like Aladdin's cave, with quantity matched by quality. Like some great but incomplete mosaic pavement the thousands of fragments shimmered under the fresh water or glistened as

they dried in the sunlight, the glossy black of the Greek paint contrasting sharply with the orange-red hues of the natural clay. Here there were rims, handles, bases, and body fragments from a host of pottery vessels used by the Greeks of more than two thousand years ago: drinking cups with one or two handles, bowls for mixing wine and water (the Greeks drank their wine diluted), storage jars, water pitchers, wine

These two drawings, a bacchanalia (at top) and a battle with centaurs (above), were also made by Tischbein from Hamilton's vases.

jugs, perfume bottles, women's trinket boxes, oil flasks. The overwhelming spread of shards washing and drying reproduced the seabed's confusion of patterned and plain, black-figured and red-figured fragments: a glorious jumble of men's and women's heads, arms, legs, feet, hands, folds of drapery, and a multitude of floral patterns—each bit a tantalizing glimpse of scenes created by Greek vase painters of centuries ago.

The date range of the pottery overall goes from the seventh to the fourth centuries B.C., but most of the shards come from painted vases made in Athens in the fifth century B.C. or in the Greek colonies of southern Italy in the fourth century B.C. Of the decorated fragments, most are in the red-figure technique, that is, the figures of the scene were reserved in the natural color of the clay and the background was painted, so that the "paint" would fire a glossy black to contrast richly with the orange-red of the figured scene. The subjects of the scenes painted on the vases were either drawn from everyday life, giving a precious insight into Greek contemporary life, or were inspired by the myths and legends of heroes and gods with which Greek literature abounds. Many individual fragments are still richly colored in spite of nearly two hundred years of tossing on the seabed; many, too, are exceptional for the quality of the drawing.

We see glimpses of young athletes in the public bathhouse washing and scraping themselves with strigils after exercise; women making a sacrifice at an altar; a woman with her workbasket; young men with wreathed heads and lighted torches dancing their way home to the tune of a flute girl's pipes after a night's gay revelry; men reclining on couches at a dinner party; satyrs chasing maenads. Among the mythological scenes we recognize the great battle between the gods and giants, and Athena, the patron goddess of Athens, with her warrior's helmet, spear, and snake-fringed aegis, watching Bellerophon on the winged horse Pegasus, which she had helped him to catch, attacking the monstrous Chimera—a story beautifully told by Pindar in one of his odes.

Outstanding among them all so far must be the group of fragments, now grown to forty-five, that shows the intoxicated smith-god Hephaestus in the company of Dionysus, the wine god, and reveling attendants. These fragments, now making up nearly a half of the main picture, come from a wine-mixing bowl, a bell krater, that was made in Athens about 440 B.C., at the time of her greatest artistic and cultural achievement, the time when Pericles was building the Parthenon. This superb scene caught Tischbein's eye, and it was copied at life size in the third volume of the Tischbein folio illustrating Hamilton's vases. Now these beautiful frag-

By 1777, when this portrait of Sir William Hamilton was made, the British Museum had acquired his first collection of antiquities. In the foreground of the portrait is one of the gems of that group, the water jar opposite. Equally splendid, perhaps, were the pieces from his second collection that went down with the Colossus.

ments may be placed on a copy of the eighteenth-century drawing; to be able to compare the rediscovered original with the drawing is an experience almost beyond our wildest dreams.

The rediscovery of the Hamilton vases, long thought lost forever, is an outstanding achievement and one that has already attracted worldwide interest. To enable this important excavation to continue, the trustees of the British Museum have decided to give generous financial support. During the winter the fragments were brought to the museum for study and further conservation. Already the final total for the 1975 season —8,186—has been unpacked at the museum, sorted, and individually marked. Now work is beginning on identifying the clay fabrics and so distinguishing the vases made in Athens from those made in the Greek colonies of southern Italy, and separating out rim, handle, and base fragments as a means of estimating the total number of vases once stowed in the *Colossus*. Detailed work on the five volumes of Tischbein's publication suggests that approximately 180 vases may have been lost in the

wreck, but already the excavation has produced fragments from vases not drawn, and thus the final total may be higher.

It is, of course, Tischbein's work that will now come into its own once more. In recent years classical scholars and particularly specialists in Greek vase painting have incorporated the evidence of the drawings into their various classifications of Greek vase styles and periods. Some of the drawings have been considered so accurate as to enable attribution of the vase from which they were copied to the style of individual artists working in Athens and southern Italy in the fifth and fourth centuries B.C. Now we will be able to check these attributions and to make many more. But this is to look into the future. First we shall use Tischbein as the indispensable tool, as the unique key to an ever-increasing number of archaeological jigsaw puzzles. For as we sort through the fragments—a process repeated time and again—individual shards may call to mind one of the drawings and may then be matched against it. Groups of fragments, either joining each other or—another enthralling game!—"floating," can be assembled so that gradually the full picture builds up. But as yet we have no complete vase or an entire painted scene from one. Nevertheless, there are high hopes that all the missing pieces may be found and that eventually it will be possible to rebuild the broken vases.

When Sir William Hamilton despaired of the salvaging of his lost vases in 1799 he wrote: "But come to the worst I have had the precaution of publishing the best that are supposed to be lost, and I have many living witnesses that the originals existed." Soon the originals may exist once more. □

Ann Birchall is an archaeologist and the assistant keeper of Greek and Roman antiquities at the British Museum.

A water jar painted by the "Meidias Painter," about 410 B.C.

SIR WILLIAM HAMILTON
An eminent scholar, diplomat, and connoisseur of art, Sir William, far left, wears the robes of a knight of the Bath in this 1775 portrait. Cuckolded, he is a ludicrous old "Cognoscente contemplating ye Beauties of ye Antique" in James Gillray's 1801 caricature.

EMMA HAMILTON
A lovely courtesan in an hour of triumph, Emma was portrayed, right, by George Romney in 1791, the year she married Sir William. Gillray's 1801 *Lady Hamilton as a Lyoness* mocks her increasing girth and lowly origins: her father was a village blacksmith named Lyon.

HORATIO NELSON
Bedecked with medals, England's greatest naval hero, Lord Nelson, far left, appears much idealized in an 1802 portrait. Gillray's *Hero of the Nile*, sketched in 1798, takes acid note of Nelson's scars, want of teeth, and unprepossessing looks.

The Life and Loves of Lady Hamilton:
A Melodrama in Several Acts

In which Sir William acquires and relinquishes the prize of his collection

AN INTRODUCTION TO THE ESSAY, CONTAINING A COMPARISON BETWEEN THE WORLD AND THE STAGE

The world has often been compared to the theatre, and many grave writers, as well as the poets, have considered life as a great drama, resembling in almost every particular those scenical representations that Thespis is first reported to have invented and that have been received since with so much delight in all polite countries. Indeed, human nature often exhibits some of her best performances to a very full house in a vast theatre of time, in which are seated both friends and critics: here are claps and shouts, there hisses and groans, in short, everything ever seen or heard at the Theatre Royal.

Let us examine this resemblance in one example: the late-eighteenth-century drama in which the principal players are Sir William Hamilton, British minister plenipotentiary to the court of His Sicilian Majesty at Naples; his second wife, Emma, Lady Hamilton, a woman justly admired for her beauty; and Horatio Nelson, the well-known admiral and naval hero, and the Hamiltons' most intimate friend, whose statue still adorns the great commemo-rative column in Trafalgar Square. Each of these characters has, in the theatre of time, received a full measure of praise and opprobrium. Sir William has been portrayed as a versatile and fascinating personage: diplomat, art collector, scientist, authority on Greek and Roman antiquities—as well as the first, be it noted, to publish an account of the worship of Priapus that still subsisted in southern Italy at the time of his residency there. On the other hand, Sir William has also been held up to much public ridicule as a foolish and complaisant husband, a man undone by his collector's and priapic instincts, justly bedecked with a cuckold's horns. In the words of the rude ditty describing Lady Hamilton's predicament when Nelson sailed out to sea again:

He's gone to fight ye Frenchmen, t'loose
   t'other Arm & Eye
And left me with the old Antiques, to
   lay me down & cry

Lady Hamilton has also been judged very variously for her part in the drama. Much has been written of her "fresh, and sweet, and exquisite beauty, both in form and figure." Artists of the day paid her the tribute of painting numerous likenesses of her as the eternal feminine. Romney, Reynolds, Sir Thomas Law-rence, Mme Vigée-Lebrun, Angelica Kauffmann, Johann H. W. Tischbein, and many others contributed to the gallery of portraits that made her the most-often-painted woman of her time. Romney alone painted more than forty pictures of his "inspirer." Yet she was also caricatured and denigrated as the "notorious" Lady Hamilton, a woman as "horrid" in her later life as she had been attractive in her earlier years.

As for Lord Nelson, his greatness as a naval commander has been much applauded, but his behavior off the quarter-deck has occasioned an equal degree of abhorrence, since the record reveals him to have been not only an ingrate and a schemer but a right rotten reactionary guilty of having connived at the murder of freedom-loving men in a most un-English fashion. It is difficult to say, therefore, who might possibly deserve to be applauded as the hero or heroine of this particular piece. As it happens so often in life, the same person may represent both villain and hero: he who engages your admiration today will probably attract your contempt tomor-row. And so it is with the lady and gentlemen involved in this drama—though whether the result is a comedy or a tragedy the author leaves to the infalli-ble judgment of the reader.

By FREDERIC V. GRUNFELD

The Divine Emma

Endowed with classical beauty and abetted by an art-patron husband, Emma Hamilton sat for more portraits than any woman in history. In a work by Angelica Kauffmann, left, she is Thalia; right and opposite, she is a Grecian goddess by George Romney, a bacchante by Mme Vigée-Lebrun, Circe, and a "suppli-cant," both by Romney. As the portraits suggest, Emma had dramatic talent: the sketches below and opposite are based on her famed Attitudes—her private performances imitating figures in ancient vase paintings.

IN WHICH A CELEBRATED
GERMAN POET MEETS A GREAT
ENGLISH BEAUTY,
AND HIS ACCOUNT OF HER
REMARKABLE ATTITUDES

When the thirty-seven-year-old Goethe came to Naples in 1787, he became acquainted with Sir William Hamilton, the collector, and Emma Hart, as she was then known, the prize of his collection, who had arrived from London the year before. They invited the poet to witness a private performance of Miss Hart's mimetic talents in a series of *poses plastiques*, which were to become better known as Lady Hamilton's Attitudes and have led to suggestions that it was she who invented the modern dance. Goethe took in the situation at a glance. As he wrote in his diary:

Sir William Hamilton, who is still living here as English ambassador, has now, after so many years as an art lover, and such an extensive study of nature, found the pinnacle of all nature- and art-pleasures in a beautiful girl. He has her with him—an English girl, about twenty years old. She is very beautiful and well built [*wohlgebaut*]. He has had a Grecian dress made for her which becomes

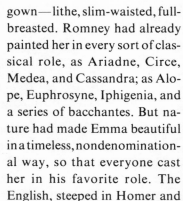

her superbly; she loosens her hair, takes a few shawls, and performs such a variety of poses, gestures, expressions, etc., that the spectator can hardly believe his eyes. He sees before him what so many artists have dreamed of painting, expressed to perfection in movements and astonishing transformations: standing, kneeling, sitting, reclining, serious, sad, playful, extravagant, contrite, alluring, threatening, and anxious. One pose follows the other and evolves into the next. She knows how to arrange the folds of her veil to suit every expression, and has a hundred ways of turning the same veils into headdresses. The old knight holds the light for her when she performs, and has devoted his whole soul to this object [*Gegenstand*]. In her he has found all the antiquities, all the beautiful profiles of Sicilian coins; yes, even the Apollo Belvedere.

Emma Hart would have been dismayed by the indignant *Vindication of the Rights of Woman* that Mary Wollstonecraft was soon to publish in London, in which she assailed the prevailing notion of woman as "created to be the toy of man, his rattle." On the contrary, Emma was delighted to be admired for her form rather than her mind. She had been born not a moment too soon to become the embodiment of the neoclassical ideal, with a Grecian profile and a figure made to order for the Empire

gown—lithe, slim-waisted, full-breasted. Romney had already painted her in every sort of classical role, as Ariadne, Circe, Medea, and Cassandra; as Alope, Euphrosyne, Iphigenia, and a series of bacchantes. But nature had made Emma beautiful in a timeless, nondenominational way, so that everyone cast her in his favorite role. The English, steeped in Homer and Virgil, saw her as a figure from pagan mythology. The Neapolitans were convinced that God had created her in the image of the Madonna. "He as been so good as to make your face the same as he made the Blessed Virgin's," she was told by one of her maids. "And . . . its true that the have all got it in their heads I am like the Virgin," she wrote, "and the do come to beg favours of me. Last night their was two preists came to our house, and Sir William made me put the shawl over my head, and look up, and the preist burst into tears and kist my feet."

CONTAINING A SHORT SKETCH OF LADY
HAMILTON'S EARLY HISTORY: A TALE
OF SO LOW A KIND THAT SOME MAY
THINK IT NOT WORTH THEIR NOTICE

It will not surprise our reader that Emma came from quite humble and, indeed, ordinary circumstances. In later

life she maintained a discreet silence about the "wild unthinking Emma" of her earliest years. Her baptismal certificate calls her Emy (Emily) Lyon, a name she later changed to the more genteel-sounding Emma Hart. Her father was a blacksmith at Neston, Cheshire, who died shortly after her birth; her mother came from Hawarden, Flintshire, and worked as a cook and dressmaker. Emma herself worked as a nursemaid in Hawarden before going to London, where, if the tale is not apocryphal, she posed as the rosy goddess of health in a "Temple of Aesculapius" run by a quack doctor who sold "nervous balsam" and administered mud baths and "electric" therapy.

By the summer of 1781, when she was sixteen, she had become the mistress of Sir Harry Fetherstonehaugh (pronounced Fanshaw), a pleasure-loving baronet who brought her to his mansion in the Sussex Downs. The house parties there are said to have consisted of a "continual succession of riotous amusements," with Emma dancing naked on the table for the benefit of Sir Harry's sporting companions. But when she became pregnant, and Sir Harry had reason to doubt that the child was his, she was sent packing. In desperation she scrawled an appeal to Charles Greville, a gentleman of a more serious

disposition, whom she had met at one of Sir Harry's shooting parties. "What shall I dow? Good God! what shall I dow?" she pleaded. "I have wrote 7 letters, and no anser. I can't come to town for want of mony. I have not a farthing to bless my self with, and I think my friends looks cooly on me. . . . O G., that I was in your posesion or was in Sir H. What a happy girl would I have been!— girl indead! what else am I but a girl in distres—in reall distres?"

A REPLY TO THE FOREGOING, AND THE MEANS BY WHICH EMMA WAS WEANED FROM DISSIPATION

The Honorable Charles Francis Greville, second son of the earl of Warwick, was a man of fastidious habits who, at thirty-three, had already seen something of the world. He had taken the grand tour, and while in southern Italy had learned a good deal about classical antiquities from his maternal uncle, Sir William Hamilton. When Greville received Emma's anguished letter, he was quite willing to rise to the occasion, provided she would give him certain personal assurances. "I will forget your faults & bad conduct to Sr. H, & to myself, & will not repent my good humor if I shall find that you have learnt by experience to value yourself," he

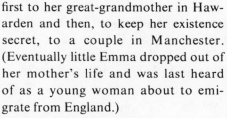

wrote to her. If she would henceforth forswear the "giddy life" and stay "clear of every connexion" (other than himself), he would agree to take her in, "give her comfort," and provide for the upkeep of the child. Emma was only too happy to comply. When "little Emma" was born three months later, she was sent, first to her great-grandmother in Hawarden and then, to keep her existence secret, to a couple in Manchester. (Eventually little Emma dropped out of her mother's life and was last heard of as a young woman about to emigrate from England.)

Miss Hart, meanwhile, was established in Edgware Row, Paddington Green, as Greville's acknowledged mistress. He became not only her lover but her teacher. He showed her glimpses of the cultivated world, improved her spelling somewhat, and brought her to Romney's studio for her first portrait. A close friendship sprang up between the painter and his model: as she wrote to him after moving to Naples, "You was the first dear friend I open'd my heart to, you ought to know me, for you have seen and discoursed with me in my poorer days, you have known me in my poverty and prosperity." She was no less grateful to Greville. He was a man of probity and good advice, which she promised she would "allways be happy to follow . . . lett it be what it will." On a visit to the seaside with little Emma she shed "tears of happiness" while thinking of all he had done for her: "Am not I happy abbove any of my sex, at least in my sittuation? Does not Greville love me, or at least like me? Does not he protect me? . . . To think of your goodness is two much."

In Which a Knight Comes to Tea in Paddington; and the Dishonorable Proposals That Are Sometimes Made by Honorable Gentlemen

It was during the summer of 1784 that Emma first met Sir William Hamilton, then fifty-four, who had come to England to bury his first wife in a churchyard on her Welsh estates. The connoisseur of antiquities was enchanted by "the Fair Tea-Maker of Edgware Row," whose profile bore such a striking resemblance to those of his favorite vase paintings. Emma, too, indulged in a certain amount of harmless flirtation. "My kind love to Sr William," she wrote to Greville in one of her letters, "and tell him if he will come soon, I will give him a thousand kisses." These signs of mutual attraction did not escape the watchful Greville, who was beginning to have second thoughts about his own relationship to Emma. His income was small; he wanted to be free to marry an heiress "of £30,000." His widowed uncle's interest in the young woman suggested a humane and mutually advantageous solution to a double dilemma. "At your age," he wrote to Sir William, now back at his post, "a clean & comfortable woman is not superfluous, but I should rather purchase it than acquire it, unless in every respect a proper party offer'd" (i.e., you would be better off with a mistress than a wife, unless she were very rich). Under the circumstances, he proposed to send Emma to his uncle on the pretext that she was to learn singing in Naples. Sir William

could be certain that she would not bring him into disrepute: "You know that from giddiness & disipation she is prudent & quiet, & that, surrounded with temptations, I have not any the least reason to complain of her."

Sir William hesitated about accepting the offer; he was less cold-blooded than his nephew and realized it would not be easy to redirect Emma's affections, "for I am sensible that I am not a match for so much youth and beauty." Besides, it might be "fine fun for the young English Travellers to endeavour to cuckold the old Gentleman their Ambassador." In the end, however, his collecting instincts prevailed. The arrangements for "forwarding" Emma were, of course, made behind her back: Greville explained to her that business would take him to Scotland for some months; meanwhile she could study music under the "roof & protection" of his kindly uncle.

In Which the History Goes Backward, to Elucidate the Character and Achievements of Sir William

Though the reader, we doubt not, is eager to know how Emma fared in Naples, we must beg him to suspend his curiosity for a short time, as we are desirous of acquainting him with the earlier events of Sir William's life, his great learning and knowledge of the world, and the distinction with which he discharged his duties as British minister to the court of His Sicilian Majesty, Ferdinand IV. Sir William's father, Lord Archibald Hamilton, had served the

Sir William (from the rear) as an antique vase: another unkind gibe

British government as governor of Jamaica and in several other posts. His mother, Lady Jane Hamilton, also served—as putative mistress of Frederick, Prince of Wales, her official title being "Lady of the Bedchamber and Mistress of the Robes." William, her youngest son, grew up at court as companion and foster brother to the prince's eldest son, the future George III, who created him a knight of the Bath in 1772. After serving in the army for a number of years, Hamilton resigned his commission at twenty-eight in order to marry, somewhat against his inclination, a "virtuous, good-temper'd woman with a little independent fortune to which we cou'd fly shou'd all other dependencies fail, and live decently." Catherine Barlow, the first Lady Hamilton, was the heiress of a very considerable fortune, said to have brought in an income of £8,000 a year. It enabled them to purchase a suitable residence, the Palazzo Sessa, when Hamilton received his appointment as envoy extraordinary to the Kingdom of the Two Sicilies in 1764.

Palazzo Sessa soon became a gathering place for lovers of art, music, and archaeology. Catherine Hamilton had studied the harpsichord, and her husband took up the violin in order to play sonatas with her—she was "considered the finest piano-forte player in Italy," according to Mozart's friend the Irish tenor Michael Kelly. She even played for the young Mozart himself and helped sponsor his benefit concert when he came to Naples in 1770. "Last night we visited the English ambassador Hamilton (our London acquaintance)," reported Leopold Mozart, the composer's father, in a letter to Salzburg. "His wife is an exceptionally expressive [*ungemein rührend*] clavier player. Having to play for Wolfgang made her tremble; she has a costly English harpsichord by Tschudi with two manuals." William Beckford, the author of *Vathek* and a relative of the ambassador's, notes in his book on Italy that Catherine Hamilton's salon was filled with artists, literati, and lovely women, but that the royal court of Naples consisted mainly of dolts, sycophants, and barbarians. The king's tutors, in an effort to avert the madness that afflicted so many of the Spanish Bourbons, had avoided teaching Ferdinand any subject that might place a strain upon the royal intelligence. (Even the fourteen-year-old Mozart was shocked to observe that "the king has been educated in the coarsest Neapolitan style.") Ferdinand's real passions were sports and hunting, and the British envoy deemed it politic to accompany the king on his periodic shooting parties. After one three-week expedition to the Apennines, Sir William reported, "We have been from morning to night without the least intermission persecuting boars, wolves, *chevreuil* & foxes, of which we have slain about 1000; 613 wild boars, some, most enormous, and very fierce."

Although Sir William's skill and endurance as a hunter gained him a great deal of influence at court, it was as an archaeologist and naturalist that he distinguished himself in Naples. He plunged into the collecting of Greek, Roman, and Etruscan antiquities with the same single-minded persistence that the king brought to his boar hunts. The market for ancient art was still in its infancy: priceless vases and bronzes could be bought from clandestine diggers and peasants who were plowing them up in their fields. During his first years in Italy he amassed more than seven hundred vases, nearly two hundred terra cottas, three hundred examples of ancient glass, some six hundred bronzes, six thousand coins, and more than one hundred gold ornaments—idols, amulets, javelins, helmets, necklaces and earrings, sacrificial instruments, and gaming dice of amber, ivory, and agate. He sold this prodigious hoard to the British Museum for £8,400 in 1772; however, in the next twenty years he went on to assemble a second great collection, mainly of vases—about a thousand of them.

Some of his treasures came from excavations that even then were being carried out under government auspices, and there are indications that he was not

The Portland vase

In his long years as envoy in Naples, Hamilton was renowned as a student of art, volcanoes, and folklore. An avid collector of ancient vases, he rightly regarded the Roman cameo glass vase above as the best in his collection. Debt-ridden, he eventually sold it to the duchess of Portland. The water color of Vesuvius above comes from the book Hamilton wrote on volcanoes.

Hamilton and friends inspect the crater of Vesuvius

Sir William Hamilton, with Emma, at an ancient gravesite

overly scrupulous about buying up pieces that ought to have gone to the Naples museum. Goethe and the painter Philipp Hackert were once shown the "secret" vault where Sir William stored his acquisitions, and Goethe wrote:

Everything was in a state of terrible confusion. Products of every epoch were thrown together at random: busts, torsos, vases, bronzes, paintings, and chance bargains of every sort; even a small chapel. Out of curiosity I pushed aside the lid of a long case on the floor; in it were two magnificent bronze candelabra. I caught Hackert's eye and asked him in a whisper if these were not very much like those in the museum at Portici. He silenced me with a look; no doubt they had strayed here from the cellars of Pompeii by a sideward path. Doubtless these and other lucky acquisitions are the reason why Sir William shows his hidden treasures only to his most intimate friends.

Sir William was equally anxious, however, that his discoveries be seen and admired by the whole world: he spent £6,000 producing a set of four elephant-folio volumes illustrating the *Collection of Etruscan, Greek and Roman Antiquities from the Cabinet of the Hon. W. Hamilton*—a work designed, as the preface points out, to pro-

vide artists with a set of "exquisite Models" and to "hasten the progress of the Arts" by helping to revive the ancient art of figure drawing. It had a palpable effect on the English neoclassical movement: Josiah Wedgwood wrote to him in glowing terms of gratitude for "the patronage you have afforded, and the assistance you have given, to the arts in this country by the introduction of so many of the valuable relicts of antiquity." Not least of these, incidentally, was the Portland vase, which Sir William bought from a collector in Rome for £1,000 (equivalent in its day to the $1 million the Metropolitan paid for its Euphronious krater) and sold to the dowager duchess of Portland for nearly double that amount; afterward it was lent to Wedgwood for twelve months to enable him to make his famous jasper ware copies of the vase.

SIR WILLIAM'S ADVENTURES WHILE OBSERVING THE ERUPTIONS OF VOLCANOES, AND OTHER PHENOMENA PECULIAR TO THE TWO SICILIES

A major eruption of Mount Vesuvius occurred in 1767, during Sir William's

Emma was thirty-three and Nelson forty when their romance began in Naples in 1798. Nelson, right, in bandages, had just triumphed at the Battle of the Nile, where he suffered a severe head wound. Emma saw him, wooed him, and won him. They are strolling, above, at Posilipo. Later Nelson hung Emma's portrait, left, in his cabin and called it his "guardian angel."

third year in Naples; thereafter the mountain that had buried Pompeii and Herculaneum fascinated him for more than thirty years. On several occasions he risked his life for the privilege of passing the night at the edge of the crater, watching the eruption. Undeterred by the fact that stones ("I dare say of a ton weight") were being hurled two hundred feet into the air and that other observers had been injured, he would approach the spectacle "as near as I could with prudence," collect samples for chemical analysis, poke at the stream of hot lava with a stick, and note the volcano's noises with a musical ear. On other expeditions he visited Etna and Stromboli; he explored hot springs, smoking craters, and lakes that exhaled noxious gases; he saw balls of fire bursting in the air and volcanic lightning that shattered the doors and windows of nearby houses; he counted the layers of cinders that had buried Roman settlements and learned what it was like to sail on a scalding hot sea that melted the pitch

from the bottom of his boat. When an earthquake shook Calabria, claiming at least forty thousand lives, Sir William was first on the scene to survey the damage and report on the phenomenon for the Royal Society in London.

Spurred on by the same insatiable curiosity, he made a trial flight into an aspect of folklore and anthropology that was to be explored in far greater depth by Sir James G. Frazer. In 1780 Sir William, by his own account, "made a curious discovery, that in a Province of this Kingdom, and not fifty miles from its Capital, a sort of devotion is still paid to Priapus, the obscene Divinity of the Ancients (though under another denomination)." At Isérnia, in the province of Abruzzi e Molise, the peasants practiced the cult of what was euphemistically known as the Great Toe of Saint Cosmo, at whose shrine the women offered up waxen votive figures "representing the male parts of generation, of various dimensions, some even of the length of a palm." The ex-voto was

kissed upon presentation of a coin. During the annual festival of the Great Toe, the canons of the church dispensed the oil of Saint Cosmo, which, according to Sir William, "is in high repute for its invigorating quality, when the loins, and parts adjacent, are annointed with it. No less than 1400 flasks of that oil were either expended at the altar in unctions, or charitably distributed, during this fete in the year 1780." This report caused a considerable furor in fashionable London, where the name of Hamilton was henceforth linked to that of Priapus. As the earl of Pembroke wrote to him from Hampton Court, "So superb a deity ought allways to have been treated with every possible mark of religion and respect."

These field trips and extracurricular activities, however, gradually turned Sir William into something of a neglectful husband. "How tedious are the hours I pass in the absence of the beloved of my heart," Catherine Hamilton confided to a diary page toward the end of her life. Her health had always been precarious; she felt herself "every day declining" while her husband spent his days leading what she was constrained to call "the dissipated life." Her death in the summer of 1782 left him duly remorseful and "quite unhinged by the cruel separation from an amiable and true friend." It was during the journey on which he escorted her body to its last resting place that he met the fair tea maker of Edgware Row.

IN WHICH WE RESUME THE ODYSSEY OF
EMMA HART, AND PERUSE THE LETTERS
CONCERNING HER PREDICAMENT
AT NAPLES

When Emma arrived in Naples in the spring of 1786, she was still unaware that she was intended to pass from nephew to uncle. Her first letters to Greville reflect her ignorance on this point. "For to live without you is impossible," she wrote. "I love you to that degree, that at this time there is not a hardship upon hearth, either of poverty, hunger, cold, death, or even to walk barefooted to Scotland to see you, but what I would undergo." At the same time she sensed that there might be more to her present situation than met the eye. "You do not know how good Sir William is to me. He is doing everything he can to make me happy. He as never dined out since I came hear; and endead, to speake the truth, he is never out of my sight. . . . I can't stir a hand, leg, or foot; but he is marking [it] as graceful and fine; and I am sorry to say it, he loves me now." Greville's only reply was to write to Sir William that he was reassured to know that Emma was in good hands.

Meanwhile she had become the belle of Naples, attended on her promenades by diplomats, noblemen, and princes of the blood. Even the king had taken a fancy to her: during a boating party he ordered his musical barge to pull alongside "and made all the French horns and the wole band play. He took off his hat, and sett with his hat on his knees all the wile, and when we was going to land he made his bow, and said it was a sin he could not speak English." Sir William saw to it that she was being suitably educated for her new role, but he must also have broken the news of what was in store for her. "I have a language-master, a singing-master, musick &c., but what is it for? If it was to amuse you, I should be happy. But, Greville, what will it avail me? I am poor, helpless and forlorn. I have lived with you 5 years, and you have sent me to a strange place, and no one prospect, but thinking you was coming. [But] I was told I was to live, you know how, with Sir William. No, I respect him, but no never."

When Greville wrote to her at last, it was only to encourage her to submit to his uncle—a suggestion that was indignantly rejected: "As to what you write to me, to oblidge Sir William, I will not answer you. For, oh! if you knew what pain I feel in reading those lines where you advise me to W[hore]. . . . Nothing can express my rage! I am all madness. . . . you, that used to envy my smiles! How, with cool indifference, to advise me to go to bed to him, Sir Wm!" By October, however, Emma had gracefully accepted the inevitable, and Greville

could congratulate his uncle on his tact: "I know that you owe your present situation to your attentions, & not to any unfair advantage, & on her part there can be no plea but free choice." Emma had talked of suicide and murder, but once the crisis had passed, she was quite willing to continue writing to Greville "on the footing of a friend."

A SHORT SKETCH OF THE DOMESTIC FELICITY THAT MAY ATTEND COUPLES WITHOUT THE BENEFIT OF CLERGY

It was now Sir William's turn to receive Emma's love letters. In December she wrote to him, while on a hunting party: "Certain it is I love you & sincerely & endead I am appreensive two much for my own quiet, but lett it be. Love as its pleasures & its pains; for instance, yesterday when you went a whey from me, I thought all my heart and soul was torn from me, and my greif was excessive I assure you; to-day I am better." Sir William, in any case, seldom strayed very far from Emma's side. His country villa at Posilipo, bought with Catherine's dowry, was renamed the Villa Emma. They were seen together at the opera on gala nights (when all seven tiers of boxes were illuminated with mirrors and candles), with Emma wearing a new gown and a hat imported from Paris, "all white fethers." Naples was then, after Paris, the second most populous city on the Continent and also a major center of the visual arts. Fifteen months after her arrival nine portraits of Emma had been completed and there were two a-painting; one sculptor was busy cutting her head in stone, another portraying her in clay, a third modeling her in wax. By general agreement no one had ever seen such a *bellissima creatura*. She learned to speak fluent Italian and passable French. When she sang— duets, arias, and ditties—people did not stop applauding for ten minutes. Her music master called it the voice of an angel: "Sir William shuts his eyes and thinks one of the *Castratos* is singing."

Together they perfected her performance of the Attitudes that had excited

Goethe's admiration. The pantomime rarely failed to please, though some of their more snobbish English guests would have preferred her to remain entirely silent during the performance. Lady Holland noted in her journal: "Just as she was lying down, with her head reclining upon an Etruscan vase to represent a water-nymph, she exclaimed in her provincial dialect: 'Doun't be afeared Sir Willum, I'll not crack your joug.' I turned away disgusted." But Emma had the satisfaction of seeing twenty-five of her Attitudes "faithfully copied from nature" by the artist Frederick Rehberg and published in several editions of etchings as "a useful study for Amateurs." Meanwhile she helped Sir William with his volcanic studies, and the delighted knight found that his student exceeded all expectations. "Our dear Em. goes on now quite as I cou'd wish, improves daily, & is universally beloved," he confided to his nephew. "She is wonderfull, considering her youth & beauty."

A SOMEWHAT SHORTER SKETCH OF THE FELICITY THAT ACCRUES TO COUPLES FROM BEING MARRIED LEGALLY

After living for five years, as she said, "with all the domestic happiness that's possible," Miss Hart and Sir William went on home leave to London, where they were joined in wedlock at Marylebone Church. The groom was sixty-one; the bride twenty-six. Romney, who pined for his model, painted the last of his portraits of her on this occasion, as "The Ambassadress." Although George III had given his consent, Queen Charlotte refused to receive the new Lady Hamilton at court—a snub that was to create an awkward protocol situation on their return to Naples, whose queen, Maria Carolina, could not formally receive any foreign lady who had not been presented to her own sovereign. Though the rule was never actually waived, Maria Carolina chose to befriend Emma in an informal way, for soon there were more important matters to concern the court of Naples.

The French Revolution swept the senior branch of the Bourbons out of office —an event particularly horrifying to Maria Carolina, since her own sister, Marie Antoinette, lost her head in the process. Europe was plunged into war, and the Mediterranean became of vital strategic interest to both England and France. As the wife, if not the official hostess, of the all-important English ambassador, Lady Hamilton was given a warm welcome. "I have been receved with open arms by all the Neapolitans of booth sexes . . . ," she wrote to Romney. "How gratefull now, then, do I feel to my dear, dear husband that has restored peace to my mind, that has given me honors, rank, and, what is more, innocence and happiness." Sir William's feelings seem to have been rather more subdued. He took pride in having rescued Emma from a moral precipice and wrote in a letter to Horace Walpole, "It has often been remarked that a reformed rake makes a good husband. *Why not vice versa?*"

─────── ❦ ───────

IN WHICH THE ARRIVAL OF A MAN-OF-WAR PUTS A DIFFERENT COMPLEXION ON A TROUBLED SITUATION, AND THE DISASTERS THAT BEFELL SIR WILLIAM'S VASES AND OTHER PROPERTY

In 1793, to signalize the new treaty of friendship between Britain and the Two Sicilies, His Britannic Majesty's ship *Agamemnon* paid a formal visit to the port of Naples, and her commander, Captain Horatio Nelson, was offered the hospitality of the ambassador's residence. That was the beginning of the intimate and enduring friendship that Emma was to refer to as *Tria Juncta in Uno*, a *ménage à trois* of which she became the prime mover. But the full flowering of this relationship was reserved for the later phases of Nelson's Mediterranean campaigns, after he had lost an eye during the capture of Calvi, an arm at the assault on Santa Cruz de Tenerife, and been wounded in the

forehead while winning his great victory over the French at the battle of the Nile. The logistics of that victory owed a great deal to Emma's behind-the-scenes manipulations. The kingdom of Naples, in a change of course, had formally adopted a policy of neutrality and nonintervention. As Nelson afterward testified, his fleet could not have intercepted the French in Egypt "had not Lady Hamilton's influence with the Queen of Naples caused letters to be wrote to the Governor of Syracuse, that he was to encourage the fleet to be supplied with every thing, should they put into any port in Sicily. We put into Syracuse, and received every supply; went to Egypt and destroyed the French fleet." In September, 1798, on the eve of his fortieth birthday, Lord Nelson sailed into Naples on his flagship, the *Vanguard.* "Alongside came my honoured friend . . . ," he wrote to his wife in England. "Up flew her Ladyship, and exclaiming, 'O God! Is it possible?' she fell into my *arm*." This was to be the last and best-remembered of Lady Hamilton's Attitudes.

Though Naples hailed Nelson as *Nostro Liberatore*, the French counterattacked on land, routing the *opera buffa* army that Ferdinand had sent against them at Nelson's behest. The royal family and some two thousand members of the court, including the Hamiltons, fled the capital aboard Nelson's ships and took refuge in Palermo, Sicily. In their absence the Parthenopean Republic was proclaimed in Naples under French protection; its chief supporters were the educated nobles and Jacobin intelligentsia. Within five months, a counterrevolutionary force under Cardinal Ruffo had fought and plundered its way from

Calabria to the gates of Naples, and Cardinal Ruffo, acting in Ferdinand's name, arranged for a republican surrender under generous armistice terms aimed at a reconciliation of the Jacobins and the royalists.

At the outbreak of the war Sir William had tried to save his second great collection of antiquities, but during his exile at Palermo he received the shattering news that the *Colossus*, with eight cases of his vases in its hold, had been shipwrecked in the Scilly Isles on the way to England. "I fear none will be recovered," he wrote to Greville, "& it is a pity, for never in this world will such a collection be made again." Though most of his paintings and some of the vases were still in Palermo, his houses in Naples had been ransacked during the civil war. He was sixty-nine; he had rheumatism and his liver was giving him trouble; he would have liked to return to England—"I feel old age coming on fast." But this was not the time to desert his post: "Lord Nelson lives in the house with us, & all business, which is immense, is transacted in our house." Besides, "I love Ld Nelson more & more— his activity is wonderfull, and he loves us sincerely."

In June, 1799, when Nelson sailed his new flagship, the *Foudroyant*, into the harbor of Naples, he was accompanied once more by both of the Hamiltons, though there was no precedent for taking an ambassador's wife into a combat zone. The queen, relying on her influence with Nelson, had appointed Lady Hamilton her "deputy," with instructions to encourage the admiral to "treat Naples as if it were an Irish town in a similar state of rebellion." Nelson needed no urging to violate the armistice and to carry out the queen's vendetta against the rebellious nobles. Some fifteen hundred republican prisoners surrendered their forts under the impression that they would be allowed to sail for France or return to their homes unmolested; instead they were herded aboard prison ships and handed over to royal-

This gold locket is engraved with the notorious codicil to Nelson's will, offering Lady Hamilton as a "legacy to my King and Country."

THE PORTSMOUTH ROYAL NAVAL MUSEUM, ENGLAND

ist star chambers for mass executions. Only about five hundred were eventually permitted to sail to Toulon. As Stendhal summed up the episode a few years later, "By the hand of her public executioner, Naples lost almost every single man of distinction among her citizens." The former commander of the republican navy, Prince Caraccioli, was brought aboard the *Foudroyant* as a prisoner of war, tried by Neapolitan officers without a defense counsel or the right to call witnesses, and condemned by three votes to two. Nelson confirmed the sentence within the hour and ordered the prisoner hanged from the yardarm at five o'clock the same afternoon and his body thrown into the sea at sundown —an action Charles James Fox was to denounce in the House of Commons as an atrocity. For Lady Hamilton, however, it was a moment of personal triumph. With the *Foudroyant* as her floating headquarters, she armed the *lazzaroni* of the city's slums to serve as execution squads, exchanged lists of the condemned with the queen, and conducted a vendetta of her own among former ladies in waiting.

IN WHICH SIR WILLIAM IS RECALLED, AND WHAT CAN COME OF VISITING ABOARD FLAGSHIPS

Word of the Nelson-Hamilton entente had reached the Foreign Office in London, and it was deemed advisable to replace the minister plenipotentiary with a younger, less encumbered ambassador. "The Queen is realy so fond of Emma that the parting will be a serious business," Sir William declared. Lord Nelson had become so fond of her that he could not part at all, but accompanied them to London by an overland route that took them to Vienna, Prague, and Hamburg along the way. When they arrived in England five months later, the second viscount Palmerston noted with

Nelson died in a blaze of glory; his Emma followed ten years later in a haze of alcohol. In this sentimental engraving of a later day, a group of classical mourners gathers around the hero's tomb.

JULIA FRANKAU, *The Story of Emma, Lady Hamilton,* 1911

surprise that Emma had grown much bulkier than he remembered her from Naples: "She was dressed in a white wrapping gown which made her look of very large dimentions, but so completely took away all shape that I cannot judge what her figure would be in a common dress." She was, in fact, about to give birth secretly to Nelson's daughter Horatia, whose existence Sir William managed to ignore. He was concerned only that "my last days should pass off comfortably and quietly." He sold some of his paintings in order to pay his debts, and when he came to take stock of his effects found that some of the vases destined for the *Colossus* had been loaded aboard the *Foudroyant* by mistake: he was able to sell the residue of the collection for £4,000. It was to be his last pleasure. He died in 1803, with Nelson and Emma at his bedside. He left her an annuity of £800 a year; the bulk of his estate went to Greville. There was a codicil to the will: "The copy of Madame Le Brunn's picture of Emma in enamel, by Bone, I give to my dearest friend Lord Nelson, Duke of Bronte, a very small token of the great regard I have for his Lordship, the most virtuous, loyal and truly brave character I ever met with.

God bless him, and shame fall on those who do not say amen." Mme Vigée-Lebrun, who had painted Emma's portrait in Naples, met her in London shortly after Sir William's death. "She said to me, with tears in her eyes, that she was deeply to be pitied; that she had lost in Sir William a friend, a father, and that she would never be able to console herself."

IN WHICH THE HISTORY IS CONCLUDED

Emma's happiness with Lord Nelson clearly took precedence over her grief, but that, too, was short-lived. With his last breath at Trafalgar, in 1805, Nelson bequeathed "Lady Hamilton and my daughter to my country." It was a legacy the nation refused to honor, and the rest of her history is a particularly unhappy version of the shabby trick that age plays on a woman whose face is her fortune. Her two final scenes, in debtor's prison and in her last alcoholic exile with Horatia at Calais in 1815, were like something out of Hogarth.

Perhaps the tale of Emma Hamilton is a morality play, like *The Rake's Progress*: if so, the feminist sisterhood should erect a monument to her as the archetypal victim of male chauvinism, a sacrifice to the cult of Priapus. Perhaps it is really a commedia dell'arte of the sort that used to flourish in Naples. Certainly she herself played the comedy through to the end with courage and style. Mme Vigée-Lebrun invited her, in her last years, to give a farewell performance of the Attitudes before an audience that included the duc de Bourbon. Though "this Andromache . . . had become dreadfully stout" and consumed several bottles of porter at a single sitting, her performance was as exciting as ever. "She passed from misery to joy, from joy to terror, so well and so quickly that we were all delighted with her." It was the story of her life. □

The Merchants of Death Revisited

Krupp was a piker compared with today's arms traders,
now operating under government auspices to ready us for World War III

In 1906 a concerned British patriot, H. H. Mulliner, just back from a business trip in Germany, brought some disquieting news to the British Admiralty. Krupp, the great German steel and armaments firm, had—according to Mulliner—recently built several huge new machines to tool gun mountings for battleships and with them could turn out a fully equipped dreadnought in six months, instead of the usual eighteen. Unless Britain, hitherto the unchallenged mistress of the seas, speeded up her own battleship program, a deadly surprise was in store for her. By 1912 Germany would have an ultramodern battle fleet that would be far superior to that of Great Britain.

The British Admiralty concluded that Mulliner's estimate of the number of "secret dreadnoughts" the Germans were capable of launching in the next six years was unduly alarmist; they felt Mulliner might be a trifle biased, for, as it happened, he was the managing director of the Coventry Ordnance Works, which specialized in mountings for big naval guns.

Convinced, apparently sincerely, that the national defense establishment was in the hands of blockheads, if not traitors, Mulliner launched a publicity campaign about the threat of Germany's "secret dreadnoughts." Soon there were speeches and sermons, even novels and plays, about the coming invasion of England by the German army after the secret dreadnoughts had done their fiendish work.

In 1909 the Liberal government, attempting to quell the controversy, ordered four new battleships to be laid down at once; the Tories counterattacked with the slogan "We want eight and we won't wait." In the end the government gave in, and eight it was. The decision, a significant milestone on the road to Armageddon, naturally provoked a speedup in German naval expansion, as well as a growing conviction in German officials' minds that England had become an unappeasable enemy.

• • •

Up to a short time ago the Mulliner affair might have seemed only marginally relevant to the problems of war and peace in the thermonuclear age. Generally neglected by sophisticated historians, arms-trade scandals of the pre-1914 era have a strong period flavor, redolent not so much of the epoch in which most of them actually occurred as of the 1920's and early 1930's, when they were dredged up by pacifist propagandists campaigning for general disarmament. To the disarmament crusaders, especially those with a left-wing bias, the whole history of the armaments industry proved that wars began essentially in the pocketbooks of the "merchants of death"; take the profit out of war and wars would cease. The investigations of the international arms trade carried out in England in 1934–36 by a royal commission and in the United States by Senator Gerald Nye's Munitions Investigating Committee helped popularize this simplistic mythology.

In the last four or five years, however, a startling change has taken place in the general world situation, and the scandalous history of the international arms trade, once a subject exploited mainly by cranks and revolutionary agitators,

has acquired a grim new relevance. To start with, there is what future historians may well look back upon as the supreme scandal of our age: the accelerating increase—and rate of increase—of military spending for the entire world. The annual figure, which stood at the appalling level of $300 billion in 1975, has been mounting rapidly (even in terms of constant dollars) every year since about 1970, according to a recent study prepared by Ruth Leger Sivard, a former chief economist of the U.S. Arms Control and Disarmament Agency. More than half of the 1975 total is accounted for by the combined military budgets of the United States and the Soviet Union, but the steepest rises occurred in the budgets of the developing nations of the Third World, where a substantial portion of the overall military expenditures was for the purchase of sophisticated weapons from the industrialized powers, mainly the United States, the USSR, France, and Great Britain. U.S. foreign military sales alone, according to other studies, amounted in fiscal 1975 to $9.5 billion—a little more than the value of the total arms trade for the whole world only two years earlier. And this despite the end of the war in Vietnam. Finally, capping this unprecedented "boom in the death business," as Emma Rothschild has characterized it, there are the revelations of global corruption—likewise on an unprecedented scale—practiced by Lockheed and other leading American producers of military aircraft. (The same unabashed bribery of foreign politicians and government officials is, of course, practiced, though generally less

Hot Sellers, 1914 and Today

German dreadnought

French-75 machine gun

British Maxim gun

Russian Foxbat fighter

French Mirage fighter

U.S. Hercules cargo plane

lavishly, by most of Lockheed's European competitors.)

All those governments buying all that death . . . And all those death makers or marketers vying with one another by offering their "contacts" de luxe vacations, automobiles, call girls, private planes; by providing furs and jewels for wives; by helping company executives keep their mistresses in style; and by filling dishonest generals' numbered Swiss accounts. All that, so those same governments—governments often unable to buy food for their own people—will go on buying more—and more sudden—death. Could the disarmament crusaders of the twenties and thirties have been on to something after all? Were they not right to put so much emphasis on the evils of the arms trade?

•   •   •

The manufacture of weapons for sale or exchange antedates history itself—Neolithic spearheads produced in France have been unearthed as far away as modern Czechoslovakia—and some of the moral or practical problems later arising out of this traffic were foreshadowed at least as far back as the Middle Ages. The crossbow, for example, was regarded as such a fiendishly lethal device that it was outlawed by a Lateran council in 1139, and firearms, though said to have been invented by a German cleric a couple of centuries later, fell under similar censure. (The chivalrous spirits of the age considered guns unsporting as well as un-Christian.) Both kinds of weapons, however, later became standard equipment among the

military forces of Christian Europe, and a prosperous industry grew up to meet the demand for them, along with that for more traditional arms.

Liège was the most important center of the arms industry, save for a brief period in the second half of the fifteenth century when Charles the Bold, duke of Burgundy, ordered the local armorers' guild to desist from further production or sales of weaponry. Charles's chief motive was probably to keep the Liègeois, who were restless under the Burgundian yoke, from arming themselves for rebellion, but he also must have chafed at Liège's trade of arms and armor with his enemies. When the guild flouted his edict, he felt strongly enough about the matter to raze the city and massacre a large number of its recalcitrant inhabitants. Before long, however, Liège was rebuilt, and the arms trade was booming again: when the duke of Alba invaded the Netherlands in 1576 the Liègeois artisans had the satisfaction of knowing that their Dutch or Flemish kinsmen, as well as the Spanish invaders, were armed with the latest weapons from Liège. The moral uneasiness that arises from making money by simultaneously arming two enemies for more efficient mutual slaughter has never ceased to haunt the trade.

But the great scandals of the arms trade occur when the trader turns out to have armed future—if not present—enemies of his own country. During the early years of the French Revolution, private concerns in supposedly hostile German states supplied the revolu-

tionaries with cannon smuggled through neutral Switzerland. A little more than a century later (not that there had been any dearth of similar cases in between) the German gunboat *Iltis*, participating in the expedition to suppress the so-called Boxer Rebellion in China, suffered damage and heavy casualties from a Chinese shore battery equipped with quick-firing cannon made by Krupp. "This is no time," the All Highest wired his friend Friedrich Alfred Krupp, "when I am sending my soldiers into battle against the yellow beasts, to try to make money out of so serious a situation."

The First World War produced a gruesome harvest of similar cases on a vaster scale. Thousands of Allied troops slaughtered in the Gallipoli campaign were hit by shellfire from British-made guns that had been sold to Turkey shortly before the outbreak of hostilities. On the other hand, British artillery throughout the war killed many more German soldiers than it otherwise could have done had not Krupp sold Vickers, the British munitions firm, the blueprint for an improved time fuse—in return for a royalty of a shilling apiece. When the United States entered the war, our navy, as the Nye committee was later shocked to discover, became the target of German submarines equipped with numerous devices perfected in American shipyards; conversely our battleships were girdled by extra-hard armor plate made by Krupp and sold by an Anglo-German-American consortium.

The classic excuse of the merchant of his own countrymen's death is the one Krupp gave the kaiser: How could he know that today's friendly customer would be tomorrow's enemy? In a period of rapidly shifting power the excuse has some validity. Occasionally a government may even encourage national arms makers to sell their wares to an obvious potential enemy on the gamble—"calculated risk" in officialese—that the diplomatic or economic benefits will outweigh the inconvenience of perhaps butchering one's own soldiers.

The arms scandals of various sorts

that periodically erupt—especially after every major war—have a deeper source, however, than bureaucratic cynicism or private greed. Indeed, scandal is built into the very structure of the modern armaments industry and trade, for the great arms manufacturer and the modern nation-state have long been, if not close partners, then very good friends.

Whereas war making had been a state monopoly in western Europe since the end of the Middle Ages, the production and distribution of the materiel necessary for making it had been left to a large degree in private hands (though many powers also maintained state-owned arsenals or naval shipyards for their own most basic military needs). Until the second half of the nineteenth century, the private firms specializing in arms or munitions were mostly small family affairs. They produced whatever they wanted and sold it where they could. But the Industrial Revolution, the rise of nationalism, and perhaps most of all the expansionist dynamism of industrial capitalism changed the situation dramatically. The modest family gunsmith or forge master became the redoubtable Cannon King.

Alfred Krupp, the heir to a small and almost bankrupt metalworks in Essen, was the first of these new industrial monarchs to be given the epithet. He won it by ceaselessly spurring his engineers along the path of technological innovation (Krupp was the first European armament maker to produce cast-steel cannon and high-quality steel armor plate), by swallowing up both his competitors and his suppliers (coal mines in the Ruhr, iron mines as far away as Spain and Sweden), and by his ruthless sales methods. Alfred had early succeeded in converting the Prussian crown prince Wilhelm to his new steel cannon, and when the latter mounted the throne of Prussia as Wilhelm I, the fortunes of the house of Krupp began to rise too. They were helped by Alfred's success in selling his cannon to other European rulers and armies. His wares were so admired in St. Petersburg that on occasion he blackmailed the Prussian generals

into giving him bigger orders by threatening to work full time for the czar. Gradually the Prussian generals came to realize that the Krupp works, with their constantly expanding production capacity and their tireless quest for improvements, were as necessary to the German army as the army was to Krupp.

Like Krupp, though not to the same degree or in the same way, the leading

Princes of the Arms Trade

Zaharoff   *Khashoggi*

"I made wars so I could sell arms to both sides," boasted Sir Basil Zaharoff in 1933, looking back on a career that began in the 1880's when he was an agent for the British arms manufacturer Nordenfelt. Later, as a purveyor of weapons for the French munitions firm Schneider-Creusot and the British manufacturer Vickers, Zaharoff got a fixed percentage of the companies' earnings. To the Boers he sold guns that were used to kill Englishmen in the Boer War, and he sold materiel to both sides during the Russo-Japanese War in 1904-5. In World War I, the profits of Vickers soared—as did Zaharoff's. By 1917 he had interests in banks, hotels, and oil wells, and his fortune was close to a billion dollars.

If secrecy, scandal, and success are the marks of a great arms trader, then Zaharoff's modern counterpart is Adnan Khashoggi. Since 1970 he has served both Northrop and Lockheed, receiving some $160 million in commissions for smoothing deals with Saudi Arabia. Khashoggi's services do not come cheap—8 per cent commission per airplane sold—but he has "expenses," including a $50,000 contribution to the Nixon campaign of 1972. Like Zaharoff, Khashoggi has invested his profits in other ventures, such as a shipping firm in Indonesia and a fashion house in Paris. Khashoggi has never boasted of fomenting a war to improve business. Considering the times he lives in, he has never needed to.

private armaments firms in France and Great Britain grew into great industrial empires and soon became quasi-official branches of their respective countries' military establishments. The Schneider-Creusot Company in France, founded in the mid-nineteenth century by Joseph Eugène Schneider, an Alsatian banker, developed political connections that gave it a dominant voice in the Army Commission of the French Chamber of Deputies; and Schneider-Creusot was credited with generally being able to nominate the navy minister of its choice. In England the two front-running firms, Armstrong and Vickers (they merged after World War I), were less overtly political, but both worked closely with the British military bureaucracies, especially the Admiralty, and their boards of directors were well staffed with retired senior officers or civil servants.

Whether in Germany, France, England, or elsewhere, there has always been a certain ambiguity in the relationship between the great armament firms and the national governments they simultaneously serve and manipulate. The temptation of munitions makers to grease the palms of government officials has often proved irresistible. In 1912 three Krupp representatives in Berlin, including one director of the firm, were accused of having paid out the relatively modest sum of 50,000 marks (about $12,500 at current exchange rates) to eight German naval officers and 13,000 marks to one artillery officer for thousands of secret War Office documents concerning new German weapons and other sensitive subjects. As William Manchester reports in his book on the Krupp firm, some of the secret information thus acquired had been deliberately leaked by Krupp agents in Paris to work up a war scare there and thereby to generate pressure at home for intensified German military preparations. Although the Germans were outraged, the prosecution took care to limit the damage, precisely because the affair involved two sacrosanct national institutions—the Prussian officer corps and the house of Krupp. Gustav Krupp von

Bohlen and the senior Krupp directors were allowed to assert their innocence, the guilty director was fined 1,200 marks, a minor Krupp employee was sentenced to four months in jail, and the officers who had sold their country's secrets were cashiered from the service and given six months in prison. As the war minister, Josias von Heeringen unhappily explained to the Reichstag, Germany was dependent on private armament firms like Krupp because only they could maintain in peacetime the huge productive capacity that would be instantly needed in case of war, but until the German army and navy could absorb the totality of their output, the firms, on their side, were dependent on foreign orders.

To a greater or lesser degree, the same rule applied—and still applies—to the private arms industry everywhere in time of peace. It is basic to the economics of the death trade.

•   •   •

The fifteen or twenty years before August, 1914, were in some respects the most lurid period in arms-trade history. The favorite hunting grounds of the arms salesmen of the period—czarist Russia and the Balkans—were particularly suited to violence, intrigue, and corruption. When the cannon kings of the great powers were not making deals behind their respective governments' backs, their field agents were slitting one another's throats—figuratively and perhaps on occasion even literally. Intimidation, sabotage of rivals' samples, fomenting of riots and coups d'état, spreading of false news, and, of course, bribery of government officials and politicians were common practices. In extreme cases even the truth might serve as a last resort to undo a rival: one of the most picturesque villains in the arms trade, Basil Zaharoff, rose to influence in England by helping the Liberals expose Mulliner's phony war over the "secret dreadnoughts." Very little can be said with certitude about Zaharoff except that he was the archetype of the shady dealer the arms trade must have as middlemen. (His counterparts today

act as "fixers" for Lockheed and Northrop.)

For most of his career Zaharoff was a more or less free-lance arms salesman operating on a commission basis. As a young man in the 1880's he persuaded the Greek government, partly by bribery and partly by organizing an anti-Turkish campaign in the Greek press, to buy a then still experimental submarine, guaranteed to assure Greece's naval superiority over Turkey. Then, by similar machinations in Constantinople, he sold two submarines to the Turks. In the years before World War I, Zaharoff played a sinister role in stirring up strife among the Balkan nations. As a behind-the-scenes manipulator, he was undoubtedly the greatest—the Muhammad Ali of the death trade. His undercover operators in Athens alone were said to have numbered 160, including "twenty-seven convicted thieves, twenty-one professional gamblers, twenty white slavers, and eight men suspected of murder." Before the war Zaharoff helped edge Krupp out of the Russian arms industry and obtained a dominant interest in it for Vickers and Schneider. At bottom the affair was a rivalry between two international armaments consortiums, each headed by a French bank, with Zaharoff having a foot in both camps and drawing com-

---

Top Ten U.S. Arms Exporters

The United States is by far the largest arms supplier in the world today, with some $10 billion in armaments and military services sold abroad each year. Yet less than a quarter of that total is sold by the ten companies listed below: hundreds of other American firms keep the world supplied with modern weapons, reflecting the biggest boom the industry has ever seen. The sales figures below are based on contracts for fiscal year 1975.

- McDonnell Douglas, $419 million
- Grumman Aerospace, $298 million
- Northrop, $293 million
- Bell Helicopter Textron, $249 million
- General Electric, $209 million
- United Technologies, $192 million
- Raytheon, $172 million
- Lockheed Aircraft, $172 million
- Hughes Aircraft, $156 million
- Boeing, $129 million

---

missions from both. Because of his chameleonlike changes of interest, it is often difficult to pin down Zaharoff's actual role: though he was connected with Vickers for some forty years and eventually held a large, perhaps controlling interest in the combined Vickers Armstrong firm, one of its officers testifying before the British Royal Commission in 1936 maintained that Zaharoff had never been formally authorized to represent Vickers in any transaction, although until his death that year he sat quite openly on the board of Vickers's French subsidiary.

Today it seems that a large part of the world is ripe for the machinations of a Zaharoff because much of the world—notably Africa and the Near East—has become Balkanized, in a sense, not only politically but psychologically. Decolonization as it was carried out by the Western imperial powers created a swarm of new sovereignties endowed with irrational frontiers, heterogeneous populations, corrupt elites, and the jealous nationalism that was the classic trait of the pre-1914 Balkan mentality.

At least during the fifties and sixties, the global power struggle between the Western and Communist blocs, while it aggravated tensions in the Third World, may have also imposed a measure of rationality on the arms programs of the new nations, insofar as they were aligned with one bloc or the other.

Purchases of U.S. arms under our military-aid programs, for example, were in theory channeled into "real"—or supposedly real—defense needs, while acquisitions of ultrasophisticated weaponry for prestige were generally discouraged. For years the desires of sundry Latin American military dictators to dazzle—or terrify—their neighbors with the latest multimillion-dollar showpieces of the U.S. aeronautic industry were politely but firmly squelched by the Pentagon. When the U.S. government followed the dangerous practice of giving or selling arms to potential belligerents like Israel and the Arab states, or Pakistan and India, it was usually in an effort to maintain the local balance of power. The results were not brilliant—witness the Indo-Pakistani war of 1965, made possible, as John Kenneth Galbraith has said, by deliveries to Pakistan of napalm and other deadly offensive weapons. Yet one could sometimes discern in the arms trade a certain strategic logic.

In the last few years, however, rationality—even the dubious Pentagon variety—has succumbed to an increasingly reckless scramble among the industrial powers to capture as much as possible of the Third World market. In 1969 Marcel Dassault, the French armaments manufacturer, sold his newest Mirage to Peru. This fighter plane outclassed every other military craft in the Latin American skies and started a stampede among Peru's neighbors that the Pentagon could no longer resist. Today the sudden affluence of the oil-producing nations is no doubt the biggest single cause of the current arms race. Iran alone has bought $10 billion worth of U.S. arms since 1971.

The dangers inherent in the present competition among the chief arms-exporting nations for the Third World market are aggravated by their increasing economic dependence on it. In 1975, according to recently published parliamentary studies in France, the nation's armaments industry (partly nationalized, partly private) exported close to the equivalent of $4.5 billion worth of military hardware, almost double the figure (in constant francs or dollars) for 1973. Since France has largely been edged out of the NATO market by U.S., British, and West German competition, a substantial part of her arms exports is going to developing nations. Any serious decline in export sales, the studies point out, would threaten the jobs of some 75,000 French armament workers. Even more serious than that would be the loss of foreign earnings. The nation faces grave trade deficits that threaten the stability of the franc. The temptation for the French government as well as the French armaments makers to exploit the fears or ambitions of Latin American dictators and Afro-Asian potentates

Top Ten Buyers of U.S. Arms

Saudi Arabia is currently the top purchaser of U.S. armaments, but Iran, running a close second, has promised to spend an additional $10 billion in American weapons by 1980. The figures below are based on preliminary data for orders placed in fiscal year 1976.

- Saudi Arabia, $2.5 billion
- Iran, $1.3 billion
- Israel, $920 million
- South Korea, $625 million
- Switzerland, $455 million
- Jordan, $436 million
- Australia, $412 million
- West Germany, $194 million
- Taiwan, $193 million
- Yemen, $139 million

is very great indeed.

Besides helping to build up productive capacity and technology at home, foreign arms sales can serve to project the influence of the supplier over the customer nation. The more important the weapons sold, the more likely they are to constitute a subtle form of imperialism. Such sales not only make the buyer technologically dependent but also inevitably furnish the seller with valuable economic and military intelligence. It is hardly surprising, therefore, that national governments have often closed their eyes to the peccadilloes of their leading armaments firms.

Even the Soviets, whose military-industrial complex is presumably untainted by the thirst for private profit and is theoretically under the vigilant control of the top party hierarchy, have become increasingly competitive in the international arms trade. The more unsavory aspects of this traffic are allegedly handled by KGB-controlled dummy firms in Bulgaria or Czechoslovakia, and unconfirmed reports in the European press say that they have dealt with such right-wing "untouchables" as South Africa and Chile. In the West a number of shady private traders, many of them associated with some national intelligence service, indirectly help the more reputable firms dodge UN or even nationally imposed embargoes. Certain relatively industrialized nations of the Third World—notably Iran and Brazil

—perform the same service for the big arms-trading countries, while at the same time marketing their own arms.

The militarization of the Third World is by no means the only evil arising out of the arms trade, as demonstrated by the Lockheed scandals in Japan, Italy, and the Netherlands, but in the long view it is perhaps the gravest. In 1975 France offered to supply South Korea with equipment and technology for producing weapons-grade plutonium, which the *New York Times* characterized as an ominous sign pointing toward "ultimate disaster." How much the armaments industries and governments of the industrialized nations are simply pandering to a spontaneous demand for arms in the developing countries, and how much they are artificially stimulating it by ethically obnoxious means, are difficult to pinpoint exactly. But what emerged about the U.S. export of arms to the Third World in last year's Washington investigations—probably no more than the tip of the iceberg—was enough to indicate that if we are not quite back in the Balkan world of Basil Zaharoff, we are headed that way.

In continuing to tolerate the corruption and other abuses that have marked the arms trade throughout history, the governments of the arms-producing nations are not merely helping to perpetuate an ancient evil. Their irresponsible competition for markets, particularly in the Third World, leads to local arms races, aggravates the general tendency toward Balkanization that already afflicts whole areas of the world, and brings us nearer to some new, no doubt nuclear, Sarajevo. Though the history of the efforts to regulate the arms trade is not exactly encouraging, it is possible that if Washington were sufficiently sensitized to the problem, the United States, the leading international merchant of death, could control its own trade and mobilize world opinion to avert the final catastrophe. □

Edmond Taylor, a frequent contributor to HORIZON, *is writing a history of colonialism to be published sometime next year.*

ECCENTRICS OF THE WORLD

Lesley Banel loved to dress as a fruit.

Felix Bernstein walked about with a suitcase full of stones.

Wanda del Vault only talked to eggs.

Romano Tong went everywhere in a motorized shoe.

The very rich and elegant Laura Wilton never combed her hair.

Wilbur Tucket lived in a tombstone.

Georges Mercier fed his paintings.

Toko Yumashi never looked at his feet.

Snooky Desvallières wrote giant letters to his friends.

Titi Kedriakis liked to be taken for a baby.

Rudolf Panov didn't wear ties.

Jo Draper loved eccentrics.

PERSPECTIVES

BERNARD LEVIN

Why the Arts Have Jumped the Tracks

Richard Tuttle's Portrait of Marcia Tucker—*under scrutiny, above, at the Venice Biennale last year—was a single piece of wood about four inches long, unpainted and hung horizontally.*

A quotation:

"I have heard of only one poetic mode that seems entirely original. A sometime student at the Royal College of Art chose a precise point in space—the half-way marker on a Dutch dyke—and a precise instant in time—say, half-past four on a specific afternoon. Having defined these unique, unrecapturable coordinates, he arranged for another human being, a friend, to meet him at the exact given intersection of these arrows of time and place. He termed this meeting a work of art, a totally controlled modification of reality, involving the deviser and the respondent in a collaborative creation. There is something haunting to the project: a sense of the poem as the creation of a total setting, as the . . . imposition of arbitrary order on inchoate possibility."

Another quotation:

"Marconi's own earliest 'sound piece' (which, incidentally, held an unseen time element since it involved drinking beer all afternoon beforehand) was the act of urinating into a galvanised bucket from the top of a ten-foot ladder."

A third quotation:

"One of his recent choral works is a 'hymn of praise' consisting mainly of the tape-recorded cries of donkeys, apes, seagulls, dogs, cats, sheep, horses, cattle, parrots, bees, ducks, elephants, lions and turkeys. Schnebel, who is a convinced Marxist and a strong supporter of West Germany's rebellious left-wing students, has also managed to introduce politics into his sacred music. At the climax of the 'hymn,' a voice emerges from the indescribable tumult of animal noises, shouting repeatedly 'Ho, ho, ho.' It is left to the singers to ad lib additional words—possibly Chi Minh."

A fourth:

"He collects thousands of old shoes, sprays them silver and scatters them in a trail across the landscape: Hungerford Bridge was one site, and the Bradford moors another. The effect of the shoe sculptures is fragile but moving because through cast-off waste one wonders about the people who wore the shoes and where their steps led them; and because the sprayed paint is both glamorous and tawdry it makes the lives of those people seem both pathetic and brave."

• • •

For every one of these four passages of modern criticism of modern modes of art it would be possible to find fifty more, or indeed five hundred, all readily interchangeable, and all characterized by the same ready abandonment of the critic's primary function: judgment. (All the quotations are from reputable critics, writing in serious newspapers and magazines. Indeed, the most preposterous of all—the one that discovered the poetic imposition of arbitrary order on inchoate possibility in a man going for a country walk in Holland—is by that modern polymath and totem figure Dr. George Steiner.)

Now it is obvious that the state of criticism must be, allowing for a time lag, a reflection of the condition of the arts themselves; it could hardly be otherwise. And if I thus reverse the natural order of things and begin with the criti-

---

Beginning herewith, HORIZON *will feature three regular columnists: Bernard Levin, a commentator for the London* Times, *who will challenge some cherished assumptions about the cultural world we inhabit; Charles L. Mee, Jr., who continues to review new books dealing with the history of our time; and John Pfeiffer, our link between the "two cultures," who will report on recent developments in science, archaeology, and anthropology that reveal us to ourselves.*

cism rather than its subject matter, it is to draw attention to what seems to me to be the root cause of the aesthetic disaster that has overtaken our world: the belief that anything is as good as anything else. That, to be sure, is not an entirely modern doctrine; Jeremy Bentham, the founder of utilitarianism, said at the end of the eighteenth century that "pushpin is as good as poetry." But for a century and a half after Bentham coined his fatuous aphorism, the world proceeded upon the assumption that Bentham was wrong, which of course he was. Only within the last two decades have we begun to persuade ourselves (for reasons as understandable as they are disgraceful) that he was right. But he was wrong, for all that.

What is under assault, and has been almost entirely overthrown, is the concept of *excellence*. The word comes from the verb "to excel," which means, after all, "to be better than," and the modern doctrine that nothing and nobody ought to be, or even is, better than anything or anybody else is not, alas, confined to the arts. The lunatic excesses of political egalitarianism, which in some forms now attributes even intellectual and physical skills and abilities to environment (there really are people who believe that *anybody*, given a sufficiently comfortable upbringing, can run a mile in four minutes or play the piano like Artur Rubinstein), pose a more serious problem than does the collapse of artistic stan-

New art for the Tate Gallery: Carl Andre's bricks, above, and Barry Flanigan's folded blankets, below.

dards; but they are at bottom the same problem. Man's art has always provided man with a mirror, and art reflects man as much as criticism reflects art, so that any examination of the malaise in the arts must be by implication an analysis of the sickness that exists in society itself.

The late B. S. Johnson wrote a novel that was published not in a binding but in a cardboard box; this was because the chapters, loose in the box, could be, according to the author, read in any order, the reader being invited after finishing the work to shuffle the sections and read it again. Johnson was not what Tennyson called "a louse in the locks of lit-

erature"; on the contrary, he was widely and genuinely admired, and was well on the way to the Nobel Prize at the time of his early death. The late Yves Klein painted (if that is the right word) a series of what he called "monochrome propositions," which were canvases covered evenly with an unvarying coat of blue paint and nothing else; he also took an ordinary, large bath sponge, dipped it in a bucket of the same blue paint, stuck it upon a stick, and lo! he had produced a "monochrome proposition" in the form of sculpture. Last year Britain was briefly but richly entertained when it was discovered that the Tate Gallery, no less, had paid a substantial sum ($8,000, some said) for a pile of perfectly ordinary building bricks stacked up by the successful American artist Carl Andre. The composer Cornelius Cardew has produced works in which the performers are invited to munch sandwiches ("it is, however, up to the individual as to how he eats the sandwiches to derive the maximum emotional effect") not just during the performance but *as part of the work*. John Cage's *4' 33"* (in which the performer sits silent and immobile before a closed piano for that length of time) has become something of a modern classic, as has Robert Rauschenberg's *Bed*, which was a perfectly ordinary bed, albeit with some paint splashed on it.

As for the Great Charlatan himself: "There is a film a few minutes long by Andy Warhol showing a youth being given an injection in the buttocks by a girl. It isn't by any means meaningless." Oh, but it is. And we may as well begin to prize open the empty Pandora's box that the arts today present, to see if we can discover how they got that way.

The collapse of form, now almost complete, and apparently irreversible, is often taken to be the essence of the ruin that has come upon the arts, and those in a mood to point an accusing finger consequently point it at such pseudocomposers as Cage, such pseudonovelists as Marguerite Duras, such pseudopainters as Ad Reinhardt; but this is to mistake the symptom for

the disease. The abandonment of the rules (and there is really only one rule, which is that art is centripetal, not centrifugal, and it is the artist's duty to keep it so) has not been brought about by such people; such people have been brought about by the abandonment of the rules. What we have to know is what caused that initial betrayal.

And "betrayal" is the right word. If you go to the Arena Chapel in Padua (or to one of the dozens of books that reproduce the pictures to be found there), you will see where painting as we understood it until only a few years ago began. Giotto was born seven hundred years ago, and the series of frescoes on the lives of the Virgin and of Christ that he

Yves Klein, who dyed sponges blue (above), orchestrated the unlikely blue work below in Paris in 1960.

painted in that church marked the end of the Middle Ages and the beginning of the modern world. From that day to well past the middle of our own century there has been an unbroken apostolic-artistic succession: Giotto begat Van Eyck, and Van Eyck begat Masaccio, and Masaccio begat Mantegna, and Mantegna begat Botticelli, and Botticelli begat Leonardo da Vinci. Then another new world began, growing with absolute naturalness out of the shell of the

Andy Warhol, "the Great Charlatan himself," with some of his products

old one: Dürer straddled the two, and there followed Michelangelo, Titian, Raphael, Holbein, Rubens. Another bridge, and Rembrandt points the way forward through the eighteenth century into the glories of Turner; and Turner begat the impressionists; and all the way down to, say, Francis Bacon the scepter was passed on, in sacred trust for mankind. *And then some fool went and dropped it.*

Not only in the visual arts; you can hear Beethoven in Bartók, just as you can hear Bach in Beethoven, and Monteverdi in Bach, just as you can find the poetry of Shakespeare in that of Robert Graves, the critical insight of Matthew Arnold in the vision of T. S. Eliot, the roaring glory of Rabelais and Cervantes in Anatole France's *Penguin Island* and the bite of that in Joseph Heller's *Catch-22*. Right down to yesterday, the heritage had been preserved, the line unbroken, the succession assured. Yet now the arts have jumped the track, and the stone on the line that has derailed the train is that of randomness.

Aleatoric music; action painting; improvised drama; you might as well talk about the cold sun, the dry sea, the blind vision. ("This is hot ice," said Shakespeare, "and wondrous strange snow.") The disintegrative principle in the arts has now become predominant, but it is only a screen behind which the dreadful truth lurks hidden. For there is only one thing—one single element—common to absolutely every true artist who has ever lived, and which unites in eternal brotherhood those who have, over two and a half thousand years, produced what is, after all, by far the greatest achievement of the human race to date: the whole body of Western art. Il Giorgione and Mozart, Catullus and Dickens, Sophocles and Picasso, Donatello and Keats, Wagner and Henry Moore, Goethe and Horace, Shakespeare and Rembrandt and Beethoven—what they all have in common is the fact that they tore their creations from themselves with an effort that we ordinary mortals cannot comprehend; indeed, it is our inability to comprehend it that sets us apart, whatever our skills or talents may be, from the company of the artists. It is that effort, that holy digging in their own vitals, that labor that made them cry out in agony for rest from their self-imposed torment —and it was out of that cry and their own refusal of its plea that they fashioned their masterpieces —that has all but disappeared from the world of art today. Hark: "Any action or sound or both is valid as music as long as it is the result of some emotional stimulus and is felt by the player to be necessary to the shape of the work." And I say that that is the lie in the soul of the modern world, which thinks that it can go straight from the emotional stimulus to the artistic result and avoid traversing the terrible desert of true creation that lies in between.

Art is pain. It must be. And the rubbish that passes for art today —the lazy, effortless, casual, thrown-together, doodled rubbish—is the result of the modern world's fear of pain and demand for an anesthetic. As I have suggested, politics and economics today are bedeviled by this same cowardice too, but it is the arts that are my concern here, and, indeed, it is in the arts that the phenomenon is most visible.

And nobody will point out that the emperor has no clothes! Nobody with any artistic authority dares to call rubbish rubbish. Dares to? Nobody even *wants* to; indeed, nobody seems to understand that it is necessary so to do. That is why I declare war on a world in which art is dying because today's artists have forgotten, if they ever knew, what mountains, what oceans, what limitless forests of passion and labor must go into the creation of a work of art. When that lost truth is rediscovered, the earth will once again be peopled with real artists, who will rub their eyes as do men who have awaked from a long sleep, uneasy with bad dreams. It is to help disturb that sleep that these words of mine have been written. For those who have fashioned a desert of triviality and called it art, may the awakening come soon. □

JOHN PFEIFFER

The Tribe That Talks Peace and Makes War

Rituals of conciliation: Yanomamo tribesmen chant in unison; below, Nixon and Brezhnev share a toast.

Living together has never been easy, but once it was much easier than it is nowadays. For more than three million years members of the genus *Homo* held to a simple wilderness-band rule: stay small, and if the going gets tough move away. So long as people clustered in bands of about five families, twenty-five to thirty persons, social conflict tended to remain at a reasonably low level, especially since individuals were free to pack up and join other bands whenever tension mounted.

That course has become less and less possible during the past ten millenniums or so. As populations soared and wildernesses dwindled, chances of moving away dwindled too, and now no alternative remains but to live in larger and larger groups. This sort of togetherness is made possible through various devices, rituals, and assumptions of which we are generally unaware. One way of gaining insight into them is to look outside ourselves, for often we can see other people's cultures, like other people's children, more clearly than we can see our own.

Research under way among the Yanomamo, a tribe of some fifteen thousand villagers settled in the dense jungles of southern Venezuela and northern Brazil, provides a case in point. Napoleon Chagnon of Pennsylvania State University has just returned from a visit with the Yanomamo, whom he has been studying since 1964, when he first lived with them as a graduate student in anthropology. According to Chagnon, no other group of people anywhere devotes more energy to the life-and-death business of trying to get along together, and no other group finds the task more difficult.

But the Yanomamo are unique in detail only. They furnish a model for the basic behavior of people everywhere, for the human condition. Like their better publicized brethren, the Lebanese and the Irish—and like the rest of us—the Yanomamo live in a world of frequent peace missions and frequently broken truces. They also live with, and are generally oblivious to, the most glaring inconsistencies. For instance, throughout the jungle good clay for pottery is widely distributed, as are vines for hammocks, bamboo plants for arrowheads, and so on. Skill is also widely distributed: every village includes people who can make first-rate pottery, hammocks, arrowheads. But that is not how the Yanomamo see it. The real jungle they live in is a "cultural" jungle, an imagined land where natural resources are unequally distributed. And so the people in one village are said to have the best clay and the best potters, and they make pottery not only for themselves but for other villages, even those several days of dawn-to-dusk walking away. They do not make hammocks and arrowheads, although they could, because they have "forgotten" how—and, besides, they "lack" the raw materials. So the products are obtained from other villages that just happen to have the materials and people with the required talents.

Such fictions are maintained for the most hardheaded reason: the Yanomamo claim to want to get along with their neighbors. Viewing the jungle as if it was a place of localized abundances and scarcities creates a setting in which people need one another and can come together with items to trade in a spirit of friendship. In other words, their system of exchange and trade is really designed to keep the peace.

So peace is manmade, an artifact, but it is an easily broken artifact. For all their good intentions, for all the wisdom of their headmen and elders, the Yanomamo cannot stop fighting. At any moment close allies can become bitter enemies. During a feast a woman from village A may go off into the woods with a man from village B, or guests high on hallucinogenic drugs may accuse their hosts of stinginess or cowardice, or a few visitors remembering old feuds may be seeking a chance to settle accounts. Whatever the reason, arguments build up to the accompaniment of name-calling, goadings, and threats. The trouble may simmer down on the spot, but more often than not it escalates, and alliances begin to collapse.

At that stage the full force of tradition comes into play. The tension is too high, insults have cut too deep to ignore. Some form of violence is called for, or at least a show of violence. There are many degrees of conflict among the Yanomamo, ranging from shouted man-to-man confrontations—chest-pounding and side-slapping duels and other ritual encounters that draw no blood—to club fights that may involve half a dozen to twenty young men on a side and considerable head-bashing and that stop only when elders decide that ceremonial mayhem has gone far enough.

Such rituals have evolved as part of the Yanomamo struggle to survive, to let off steam short of war. When everything fails, when war is imminent, villagers live in a hair-trigger state of suspense and fear. People build palisades ten to twelve feet high and are constantly on the alert. Any suspicious sound in the surrounding jungle, a rustling of leaves or the snapping of a branch, is enough to make every man grab his bow and arrow and rush out ready for combat.

Things are also humming at the diplomatic level. Warriors from a village under threat of violence meet warriors of a nearby village, offering an unequal exchange of gifts: "Your gorgeous earring—it is so beautiful! I can't live without it! Here, take my ugly, worthless machete." The earring is a piece of bamboo with a feather stuck in it, the machete a highly valued object of steel—but the exchange marks another beginning, a new friendship and a new alliance and the enduring hope for security.

Meanwhile people prepare for the worst. The Yanomamo exist in a state of chronic warfare. In one region of some fifty villages, about half are engaged in some kind of fighting at any given time. The other twenty-five villages are not at peace, however. "They have enemies somewhere out there," Chagnon has observed, "and they never know when all hell may break loose." "All hell" means ambushes and sneak attacks, often at dawn's early light.

The death toll per raid is not high by our standards. An attack usually results in a single killing; two or three fatalities are exceptional. But a village may raid or be raided half a dozen or more times a year, and about one out of every four adult males dies in battle. As far as tribal survival is concerned, however, the victims are expendable. Population has been on the rise for at least two centuries.

The Yanomamo do not question their own behavior. They switch specialties whenever they switch alliances. People who had "forgotten" how to make pots and had no good clay suddenly remember the potter's art and discover clay near their village. And now they "forget" how to make hammocks or arrowheads or whatever else they had been producing for their former allies. What appears so obviously contradictory, what makes no sense when viewed from the outside, is the way of the world, "human nature," when viewed from within. The Yanomamo readily find reasons to love or to hate their neighbors. They say they want to stop fighting, to stop threatening and terrorizing and killing each other. "We're tired of fighting. We don't want to kill anymore. But"—and the qualification comes tragically in the same breath—"they are treacherous and cannot be trusted."

There is no easy explanation for the violence of the Yanomamo, or for the violence of the rest of the world. But there is a clear message. Being civilized has nothing to do with going to school or church—nothing to do with the trappings of technology, the radar ovens and minicomputers, spaceships and missiles with nuclear warheads. Being civilized is an ideal, something for the future perhaps. Right now we are all primitive. Not for nothing has man been described as the missing link between anthropoid apes and human beings. □

STATEMENT OF OWNERSHIP, MANAGEMENT, AND CIRCULATION

(Required by 39 U.S.C. 3685)

1. Title of publication: HORIZON
2. Date of filing: October 1, 1976
3. Frequency of issue: quarterly
   a. Number of issues published annually: 4
   b. Annual subscription price: $26.00
4. Location of known office of publication: 10 Rockefeller Plaza, N.Y., N.Y. 10020
5. Location of the headquarters or general business offices of the publishers: 10 Rockefeller Plaza, N.Y., N.Y. 10020
6. Names and addresses of publisher, editor, and managing editor: Publisher, Rhett Austell, 10 Rockefeller Plaza, N.Y., N.Y. 10020; Editor, Shirley Tomkievicz, 10 Rockefeller Plaza, N.Y., N.Y. 10020; Managing Editor, Priscilla Flood, 10 Rockefeller Plaza, N.Y., N.Y. 10020
7. Owner: American Heritage Publishing Co., Inc., 10 Rockefeller Plaza, N.Y., N.Y. 10020. Names and addresses of stockholders owning or holding 1 per cent or more of total amount of stock of American Heritage Publishing Co., Inc.: Engelhard Hanovia, Inc., 10 Rockefeller Plaza, N.Y., N.Y. 10020.
8. Known bondholders, mortgagees, and other security holders owning or holding 1 per cent or more of total amount of bonds, mortgages, or other securities: none
9. For completion by nonprofit organizations authorized to mail at special rates: not applicable
10. Extent and nature of circulation:

	Average No. Copies Each Issue during Preceding 12 Months	Actual No. Copies of Single Issue Published Nearest to Filing Date
A. Total no. copies printed (net press run)	106,335	103,000
B. Paid Circulation		
1. Sales through dealers and carriers, street venders, and counter sales	—	—
2. Mail subscriptions	97,850	94,820
C. Total paid circulation (sum of 10B1 and 10B2)	97,850	94,820
D. Free distribution by mail, carrier, or other means, samples, complimentary, and other free copies	210	210
E. Total distribution (sum of C and D)	98,060	95,030
F. Copies not distributed		
1. Office use, left over, unaccounted, spoiled after printing	8,275	7,970
2. Returns from news agents	—	—
G. Total (sum of E, F1, and F2—should equal net press run shown in A)	106,335	103,000

11. I certify that the statements made by me above are correct and complete.

Rhett Austell,
Publisher

12. For completion by publishers mailing at the regular rates (Section 132.121, Postal Service Manual). 39 U.S.C. 3626 provides in pertinent part: "No person who would have been entitled to mail matter under former section 4359 of this title shall mail such matter at the rates provided under this subsection unless he files annually with the Postal Service a written request for permission to mail matter at such rates."

In accordance with the provisions of this statute, I hereby request permission to mail the publication named in Item 1 at the phased postage rates presently authorized by 39 U.S.C. 3636.

Rhett Austell,
Publisher

CHARLES L. MEE, JR.

Neruda's Memoirs: *The Making of a Stalinist*

Ambassador Neruda: Paris, 1971

Pablo Neruda, who died in 1973 at the age of sixty-nine, was a great poet. His work is especially brilliant not because of its modern rhythms and structures, although his poetry is strong and sound, or because of its language, however crystalline and fiercely correct it is at times. His poetry is great for the passions it expresses, and the passions—some of the most powerful of them—are political. Neruda was at the center of his country's politics; he was a senator in Chile, and during Salvador Allende's brief administration he was ambassador to France. Neruda tried to provide a voice for the poor and the powerless, for all of his countrymen who had no voice. In doing so he became one of the great poets of our century, whose work and life are an indelible expression of our times.

When Neruda was running for the senate in 1945—he was forty-one then—he observed firsthand the plight of the copper and nitrate miners in the deserts of northern Chile. "It hasn't rained for half a century [there]," Neruda wrote in the *Memoirs* that have just been published by Farrar, Straus and Giroux, "and

the desert has done its work on the faces of the miners. They are men with scorched features; their solitude and the neglect they are consigned to has been fixed in the dark intensity of their eyes. Going from the desert up to the mountains, entering any needy home, getting to know the inhuman labor these people do, and feeling that the hopes of isolated and sunken men have been entrusted to you is not a light responsibility. But my poetry opened the way for communication."

He considered himself a public poet, and he addressed his life and his works to championing the cause of the working people to whom he was born and chose to belong. "Coming into those lowlands, facing those stretches of sand, is like visiting the moon. This region that looks like an empty planet holds my country's great wealth, but the white fertilizer and the red mineral have to be extracted from the arid earth and the mountains of rock. There are few places in the world where life is so harsh and offers so little to live for. It takes untold sacrifices to transport water, to nurse a plant that yields even the

humblest flower, to raise a dog, a rabbit, a pig."

This enormous wasteland of riches is controlled by the nitrate corporations. "The English, the Germans, invaders of every kind, took over the productive regions and gave them company names. They imposed their own currency; they prevented any kind of assembly by the people; they banned political parties and the people's press. You could not enter the premises without special permission, which, of course, very few were able to obtain." During his campaign for the senate, Neruda walked the pampa and spoke to the miners. One afternoon he talked with the workers in the machine shop of a salt mine. He stood on planks that kept him out of the water, oil, and acids that otherwise turned the floor of the shop into a mire. "Those planks," one of the workers explained to Neruda, "cost us fifteen strikes in a row, eight years of petitioning, and seven dead."

Neruda's poetry sprang from the sympathies that grew from such encounters. On another occasion, while he was visiting a coal mine on a hot and bright day, a man emerged from one of the tunnels, "as if rising out of hell, his face disfigured by his terrible work, his eyes inflamed by the dust, and stretching his rough hand out to me . . . he said to me, his eyes shining: 'I have known you for a long time, my brother.'"

On July 8, 1945, several months after he had been elected to the senate, Neruda became a member of Chile's Communist party. He became a Communist, clearly, because he was a decent man, just as so many French and Italians are becoming Communists today, feeling that they have no other choice but that between fascism and communism, corruption and communism. I had thought no one became a Communist anymore, certainly not since Stalin. But the virulence of fascism and the corruptions of democracy are giving it a revival. Although I think that more self-rule, more democracy, is what is needed—both to obtain social justice and to ensure the political

power to keep it—I do not doubt the rationality of Neruda's choice.

Certainly his commitment to communism was betrayed often enough to give him an opportunity for second thoughts. In 1946 he managed the campaign of Gabriel Gonzalez Videla, who was elected president by a large majority. "But, in our creole America," Neruda wrote, "Presidents often go through an extraordinary metamorphosis. . . . The new chief of state quickly changed his friends, he got his family into the 'aristocracy,' and was gradually transformed from a mere demagogue into a potentate." Many of Videla's old friends were packed off to jail. In the senate Neruda gave increasingly harsh speeches until, in 1948, his arrest was ordered. He went underground.

"I moved from house to house every day. Doors opened to receive me everywhere. It was always people I didn't know, who had somehow expressed their wish to put me up for a few days. They wanted to offer me asylum even if only for a few hours, or for weeks." While hidden, he wrote his *Canto General*, and it was published clandestinely.

Early in 1949, however, he and his friends determined it would be best for him to leave the country. He was to go on horseback across the mountains into Argentina. Beginning the journey by automobile—at sundown—Neruda and a companion drove day and night. Neruda sported a beard and wore dark glasses—and, bundled up under blankets when they had to stop for gas, he could hardly have been more conspicuous.

Just before they were to cross the Andes, they stopped to rest at a large lumbering estate—and then, unexpectedly, the owner of the estate arrived. Neruda decided at last to confront this man, a close friend of Gonzalez Videla, and risk arrest again. They met in the middle of the forest; the owner declared that he would personally see to Neruda's safety, and then they retired to a sparsely furnished cabin in the wilderness, drank a bottle of whiskey together, and argued furiously.

But they parted friends. Indeed, the owner called his workers together and told them to open up a road across the Andes so that the poet would not risk capture by taking the smuggler's pass. Two years later, Neruda heard that the owner had been arrested, accused of running a big smuggling operation, jailed, and had died soon after.

Seven men set out through the jungle with Neruda. They went on horseback, single file, through the giant larch and mayten and rauli trees. "I stopped to measure one. It had the diameter of a horse. The sky overhead can't be seen. Below, leaves have been falling for centuries and forming a layer of humus the hooves of the mounts sink down into." They crossed rivers, crags, and fields of snow, and "each one moved along, absorbed in that solitude without boundary lines, in the green and white silence." They went by wooden tombs of others who had not survived the passage; they crossed a torrent in which the father of one of the guides had been killed some years before. Emerging from a natural tunnel in the granite, they came upon a bull's skull. "My companions approached it in silence, one by one, and left a few coins and some food in its bone sockets. I joined them in that offering intended for rough-mannered men who had strayed away like Ulysses, for fugitives of every breed, who would find bread and assistance in the dead bull's eyepits."

In short, they crossed the Andes. Neruda was handed along from person to person, until at last he got hold of the passport of an old Guatemalan novelist friend, Miguel Angel Asturias, and with that he went to Paris.

He arrived in Paris the way I should like to arrive one day. He went first to the Hotel George V. Where else would his outrageous mountain clothes be calmly regarded as the eccentricity of a rich guest? "And then Picasso showed up. . . . He was as thrilled as a little boy, because he had just given the first speech in his life. Its theme had been my poetry, my persecution, my absence. . . .

He spoke to the authorities; he called up a good many people." He got Neruda settled in Paris.

Not long after, Neruda was brought into the Ministry of Foreign Relations and told that he was going to be deported from France for making clandestine trips to Spain at the behest of Ilya Ehrenburg, the Russian novelist whom Neruda called one of the most "ebullient of the great agitators of Soviet culture." As it happened, Neruda had never met Ehrenburg, but he knew that the Russian "went to La Coupole every day, where he lunched at a Russian hour, that is, around sundown." Neruda found Ehrenburg there. " 'I'm Pablo Neruda, the poet, from Chile,' I said to him. 'According to the police, we're close friends. . . . Since they're going to throw me out of France because of you, I wish to meet you, at least, and shake hands.'

"I don't believe Ehrenburg ever blinked at any phenomenon in the world. And yet I saw something very much like a look of stupefaction emerging from his shaggy brows, from under his angry mop of gray hair.

" 'I also wanted to meet you, Neruda,' he said. 'I like your poetry. But, to begin with, have some of this *choucroute à l'Alsacienne.*' "

In time Neruda fetched up in Moscow. "I loved the Soviet land at first sight, and I realized that not only does it offer a moral lesson for every corner of the globe where human life exists . . . but I sensed, too, that an extraordinary flight would begin from this land of steppes, which preserved so much natural purity."

Neruda's romantic attraction to Russia makes me wince; but it was not the worst of his faults. He was a Stalinist, and that is no small error to be easily glossed over. Neruda himself cannot explain it. "The report of the Twentieth Congress was a ground swell that drove all of us revolutionaries to take new stands and draw new conclusions. Many of us had the feeling that, from the anguish produced by these painful revelations, we were being born all over again. We were reborn cleansed of dark-

ness and terror, ready to continue the journey with a firm grip on the truth."

But this is insufficient. Today, when few of us believe in any leaders at all, it is galling to see Neruda trim his remarks on, of all men, Stalin. Such evasions inevitably take their toll. The poet's voice goes bad, sounds tinny and hollow, when it tries to avoid the natural response to tyranny. I can only guess that his rage against the mine owners and other economic and political dictators of Chile must have been stupendous; it distorted his life and his poetry and his feelings re-repeatedly, and it threatened to ruin him.

Neruda returned to Santiago in 1952, an order for his arrest having been revoked. For the next twenty years he wrote poetry; he won the Stalin Peace Prize; he founded and edited reviews; he traveled. No summary of all these years would suffice: these were the years of an enormously productive middle age. He toured the country during the presidential election of 1958; he wrote political poems and love sonnets; he published *The Stones of Chile* and *Ceremonial Songs*, and he began the memoirs of his childhood.

Portions of the complete memoirs, now published, are finished works that have been rewritten and polished and that are strong and evocative, intensely clear and exact. Other, later portions are roughhewn, awkward notes and scribblings. They are self-conscious and unconvincing, full of puffery and posing, bragging and preening, but I like them all, the lapses as well as the most artful pages, the flaws sometimes even more than the virtues. All of them discover an interesting character of capacious talents and appetites and passions, and they record a political odyssey of deep feeling and principle, and a final terrible ending.

In 1970 Neruda's politics and his poetry were both recognized in the most satisfying way. His political ally, Salvador Allende, won the presidential election in Chile; Neruda was appointed ambassador to France, where he served for two years, and in 1971 he was awarded the Nobel Prize.

"For one hundred and eighty years, the same kind of rulers under different labels had succeeded one another in my country, and they all did the same thing. The rags, the disgraceful housing, the children without schools or shoes, the prisons, and the cudgelling of my poor people continued. Now we could breathe and sing. That's what I liked about my new situation."

One of the mining companies tried to place an embargo on Chilean copper; Allende nationalized the copper deposits. Posters appeared on the walls in the cities—anti-Communist posters, anti-Soviet posters, anti-Cuba posters. General René Schneider, the chief of staff who had opposed a possible coup d'état to keep Allende from acceding to the presidency, was assassinated. Finally, on September 11, 1973, "Allende's home . . . was bombed from the air. . . . The tragic symbolism of this crisis became clear in the bombing of the government palace; it brings to mind the blitzkrieg of the Nazi air force against defenseless foreign cities —Spanish, English, Russian. Now the same crime was being carried out again in Chile. Chilean pilots were dive-bombing the palace, which for centuries had been the center of the city's civic life.

"I am writing these quick lines for my memoirs only three days after the unspeakable events took my great comrade, President Allende, to his death. His assassination was hushed up, he was buried secretly, and only his widow was allowed to accompany that immortal body. . . . Immediately after the aerial bombardment, the tanks went into action, many tanks, fighting heroically against a single man . . . who was waiting for them in his office, with no other company but his great heart, surrounded by smoke and flames. . . . He had to be machine-gunned because he would never have resigned from office."

Twelve days later, on September 23, Neruda died of cancer. His house in Valparaiso, as well as the one in Santiago where his wake was held, was sacked and destroyed. □

Famous Last Apothegms

A celebration of the art of dying with your wits about you

By PETER ANDREWS

"Die, sir?" said Lord Palmerston when his doctor informed him of the gravity of his physical condition. "That is the last thing I shall do!" And so it was. The English statesman expired shortly thereafter, his final words on the subject having been that simple, unassailable truth.

Palmerston lived in an age when people departing this world for what Rabelais called "the great perhaps" were expected to have something pithy to say about the experience. Modern man, having failed to banish death, seems determined to ignore it. So when the perpetual cold finally settles into our bones, it comes as a startling and unexpected development. Medical science prescribes painkillers and special machinery so that no one, including the corpse itself, can be sure that death has occurred without looking at the appropriate telemetry.

In an earlier time this would have been considered a discourtesy to so momentous an event. Sir William Davenant, the seventeenth-century English dramatist, paid death the proper respect. He begged pardon that he would be unable to complete an epic poem on which he was at work, saying, "I shall ask leave to desist when I am interrupted by so great an experiment as dying."

Sir William's line may seem a bit studied, but the spirit it showed was not uncommon. "So this is it at last," said Henry James as he suffered the stroke that was to kill him, "the distinguished thing." When Dr. Johnson was told that his case was hopeless, he was as resolute in his manner of dying as he was in his speech. "Then I will take no more physic," he told the doctor. "Not even opiates, for I have prayed that I may render my soul to God unclouded."

By modern standards, Dr. Johnson's passing would be considered painful, but it is doubtful that he would have wished to endure the more humane passing of Oliver Wendell Holmes. When he grew older, Holmes said he could hear the "roar of the cataract" but did not seem disturbed by the sound. Holmes lived to ninety-three and was ready. He watched as attendants wheeled in an oxygen tent and rigged it around his hospital bed. "Lot of damned foolery," he commented, and was never heard to speak again. Whatever last words he may have had for us were lost in the hiss of the gases he did not particularly wish to receive.

The great jurist may well have been annoyed to be denied a proper death scene, for the Holmeses were masters of leaving this world in style. The death of his uncle John was a legend in Cambridge. As the family stood around the old man's deathbed, a nurse reached under the covers to feel his feet, and told the relatives that John Holmes still lived. "Nobody ever died with their feet warm," she whispered.

Even in his final moments, Holmes's historical sense did not desert him. He looked up, clear-eyed, and spoke his last words: "John Rogers did." Rogers had been burned at the stake for heresy in 1555.

The recording of *apothegmata morientum*, the dying words of great men, was once a respected practice. It was the common custom to huddle around the deathbed of a prominent citizen in order to catch the final words and relay them to the world. Unfortunately the reporting has tended to be extremely unreliable; the people of an earlier age were not above dressing up a quote for public consumption. The death of Lope de Vega in 1635 was a national event in Spain. When the great dramatist breathed his last, his final words were reported to be: "True glory is in virtue. Ah, I would willingly give all the applause I have received to have performed one good action more."

You can believe that the author of some eighteen hundred comedies really said that if you wish. I much prefer another account, which holds that he looked up at the distinguished visitors gathered in his sickroom and sought their assurances that he really was going to die, because he had a confession to make he dared not survive. Told that the void was indeed opening before him, de Vega spoke out: "All right then, I'll say it. Dante makes me sick."

If second parties often doctored the death speeches of the mighty, the dying themselves have not always been above playing to the gallery. Joseph Addison, the great English essayist, seemed determined to make even his own death into a lesson in Christian morality. He called for his nephew to come and "see in what peace a Christian can die."

One gets the feeling that Voltaire possibly jotted down "What, the flames already?" at the first twinge and stored it away for later.

"There is nothing I seek information about as willingly as the way people die," wrote Montaigne. Indeed, we are apt to feel cheated if we don't know the manner of a hero's death. Sometimes that's all we need to know. The constable de Montmorency is hardly a household word, even in the home of a French historian, but still today, knowing nothing more about him than his last moments on earth, we can get a sense of the kind of man he was. The constable received a mortal wound fighting in the battle of Saint-Denis in 1567. When his aides rushed up to help him, de Montmorency waved them aside, saying, "I have not lived eighty years without learning how to stand dying for a quarter of an hour."

Most people try to stick to their guns the best they can when the end approaches, but I find myself drawn to men of a gentler mode who rise to the dignity of the occasion but still manage to slip away without any great fuss. All of us wish to die well, and I think the French grammarian Dominique Bouhours may have died as well as anyone. Bouhours was a man of high professional standards. When he went at the age of seventy-four in 1702, his last line was a model of professionalism: "I am about to—or I am going to—die: either expression is correct." □

de Montmorency
1493–1567

William Davenant
1606–1668

Joseph Addison
1672–1719

Voltaire
1694–1778

Samuel Johnson
1709–1784

Lord Palmerston
1784–1865

Oliver W. Holmes
1841–1935